ON MIGRATION

On Migration

Dangerous Journeys and the Living World

Ruth Padel

COUNTERPOINT

BERKELEY

First published in Great Britain in 2012 by Chatto & Windus
Typeset by Palimpsest Book Production Limited, Falkirk, Stirlingshire
Design by Richard Marston
Cover design by Attebery Design

Library of Congress Cataloging-in-Publication Data is available
ISBN 978-1-61902-433-5

COUNTERPOINT
2560 Ninth Street, Suite 318
Berkeley, CA 94710
www.counterpointpress.com

Printed in the United States of America

For Pedro, Gisa, Bruno and Mia

Contents

Acknowledgments

This book, travel for it and time to write it, was made possible by an Individual Artist's Award from the Arts Council of England for which I am very grateful. Many warm thanks also to the Environment Institute and History Department of University College, London, for a Resident Writer's Fellowship, which enabled me to finish it. Enormous thanks to David Harsent for his editing of the poems, and to Ian Pindar for his copyediting.

I have discussed migration with many people for many years and am very grateful to them all for their responses, especially those who gave their time and expertise to comment on the prose. They include Phillip Birch, Tim Birkhead, Kathleen Burke, Gwen Burnyeat, Mark Cocker, Elaine Feinstein, Eva Hoffman, Kerin Hope, Aamer Hussein, Sanjay Iyer, Sushrut Jardav, Lauro Martines, Jeremy Mynott, Michael Oberts, Sigrid Padel, Arshia Sattar and Tom Schuller. Many thanks also to people who gave material which sparked things off, especially Peter Conradi, Ruth Fainlight, Caroline Moorehead, Elizabeth Nabarro, Felix Padel and Alexa Walker.

Thanks to Susie Symes for an inspiring introduction to the Museum of Immigration at 19 Princelet Street, to Mark Baldwin for an invitation to watch Ballet Rambert rehearse and talk to the dancers, to D. V. Girish of Bhadra Wildlife Conservation Trust for guidance in the forest over many years (also for the Rufous Turtle Dove), to Andrew Morley for genetics and Claudio Scazzocchio for Lessespian migration.

I should like to thank the Wellcome Trust for a commission

to write the text for *Music from the Genome,* Somerset House Resident Writer's Programme for an invitation to talk on Bruegel's *Landscape with Flight into Egypt* at the Courtauld Gallery, and the Kate O'Brien Conference, Limerick, for an invitation to give an address on the theme of 'outsiders', which helped me shape reflections on the key figure of John James Audubon.

Thanks also to editors who published some of these poems – in *Acumen*; *Arvon Poetry Competition Winners 2006*; *Barque Bernaque (Poems commissioned by Newcastle Centre for the Literary Arts to accompany 'The Cultural Life of Barnacles' Exhibition at the Great North Museum Newcastle, 2009)*; *Best British Poetry 2011*; the *Guardian*; *Hortus*; *interLitQ.org*; *London Review of Books*; *The New Humanist*; *New Statesman*; *New Welsh Review*; *The New Yorker*; *Poetry Review* and *The Wolf*. Also to Sonja Patel, editor of the anthology *Nature Tales: Encounters with British Wildlife* (2010) where some prose passages were first published. Earlier versions of three poems appeared in my previous collections *Angel* (Bloodaxe, 1993), *Fusewire* (Chatto, 1996) and *Voodoo Shop* (Chatto, 2002).

I can't thank my editors, Parisa Ebrahimi and Clara Farmer, enough for their advice and support. Parisa's fine judgement, patience, kindness, vision and clear head made sure that whatever trees we wandered among, we never lost sight of the wood.

On Migration

Ripples on New Grass

When all this is over, said the princess,
this bothersome growing up, I'll live with wild horses.
I want to race tumbleweed blowing down a canyon
in Wyoming, dip my muzzle in a mountain tarn.

I intend to learn the trails of Ishmael and Astarte
beyond blue ridges where no one can get me,
find a bird with a pearl inside, heavy as ten copper
                                                    coins,
track the luminous red wind that brings thunder
and go where ripples on new grass shimmer
in a hidden valley only I shall know.

I want to see autumn swarms of monarch butterflies,
saffron, primrose, honey-brown, blur sapphire skies
on their way to the Gulf: a gold skein
over the face of Ocean, calling all migrants home.

Migration Made the World

You really feel the earth turn in September. The planet is sliding us into autumn. On the other side of the equator it must be sliding everyone into spring, but here every morning seems a little darker.

I come into the kitchen and see starlings round the bird-feeders outside. Dawn glows through the geisha fans of their wings as they try to eat and flutter at the same time. One of them does it by hanging upside down and sticking its tail over its head. They may live in London the whole year but they could have flown across the English Channel last night. Starlings are partial migrants – some migrate, some don't. Huge flocks arrive every autumn on England's east coast and radiate out to join other starlings across the country. In spring, hundreds of thousands go back to nest in Eastern Europe.

We were all wanderers once. We walked out of Africa looking for food, safety, water, shelter and territory. Travelling was where we began and *Homo viator*, man the pilgrim, life as pilgrimage, is deep-engrained in Western thought. Mediaeval Christianity said we were strangers in this world, searching for the spiritual homeland to which we originally belonged. We weren't meant to be here – we were put in a garden. But that went wrong and now we are wanderers between two worlds, wayfarers on the *via*, the 'way', of life.

Human beings are both fixed and wandering, settlers and nomads. Our history is the story of the nomad giving way to the settler but when people are unsettled they have to migrate. The point of migration, whether you are a starling or a human being, is to reach whatever helps you and your children live in a new place. Home and migration belong together, two sides of the same ancient coin. Home is something we make, then things change, either in ourselves or in the world, we lose home and have to go elsewhere.

The word 'migrate' covers many sorts of move. It comes from the Latin *migrare*, 'to move from one place to another', and is related to 'mutable' and the Greek *ameibein*, 'to change'. We use it for two types of journey. Both can be undertaken either by large groups or individuals on their own. The two have a lot in common, but there is a wide spectrum of activity between.

The type of migration we think of in relation to animals, though human migrant workers and commuters also do it, is a periodic and usually seasonal move and return between one place to another. I shall call it Go and Come Back. The other type, Go and Stay, is a permanent move to a new region and often takes the form of invasion and colonisation. It seems to be typically human but animals and plants do it too.

Only humans, however, go in for emigration (going permanently away from home) or immigration (coming to settle permanently in a new home). These words suggest a political boundary has been crossed. Another word to throw into the mix, sometimes used interchangeably with migration, is transmigration. It can mean moving from one place or one stage of life to another but has the extra dimension of reincarnation: the soul is moving to another body to be born again.

Underneath all this is the idea of travelling towards something you need and don't have. Migration is a process with two elements: the journey towards a new life and the settling into it. This book is about the journey.

There is a push and a pull factor to migration. The push may be escaping war or famine or a freezing winter. The pull is usually safety, warmth, food or work. But whichever is uppermost, whether the travel is cyclical like swallows in spring and autumn, or once in a lifetime, migration is about survival.

The push factor is both outer and inner. The external force compelling you to migrate may be geographical and climatic like an ice age or the arrival of a competing species. But there is an abstract way of putting these: you leave because of some loss, danger, threat or lack which triggers inner pressures that also have abstract names (though they are not experienced abstractly) like hunger, fear and hope. The great dream is of something better elsewhere. Hope of a new life is the positive force behind human migration. Hope and imagination – picturing that new life – are push and pull combined.

Seven years ago I watched the wildebeest migration from Kenya to Tanzania, whose last awful stage is the crossing of the Mara River. I wanted to hold migration up to the light from a lot of different angles and set the struggle of migration, the effort of getting there, in the context of biology and history. But after the poems were written the background seemed so complex and extraordinary that I wanted to set it out more openly too, in prose. Switching between one place and another is intrinsic to migration, so it seemed apt to go between poetry and prose, and there was a wonderful model for mixing them whose title was also appropriate for migration: *The New Life.*

The mediaeval *prosimetrum*, a literary genre which combined prose and poetry, followed sixth-century reflections on happiness by the philosopher Boethius. *De consolatione philosophiae,* written in a Roman jail before Boethius was executed by an Ostrogothic king, tells the story of his philosophical and spiritual self-discovery. Mediaeval readers loved Boethius; mediaeval writers copied his shape-shifting blend of philosophy and poetry. *Cosmographia* was an account of the creation of the universe by the twelfth-century poet-philosopher Bernard Silvestris. *The Fire of Love* was a mystic poem on Christ by a fourteenth-century Yorkshire hermit, Richard Rolle. A French form, the *chantefable* or 'song-story', mixed prose and poetry to tell stories of knighthood and courtly romance. But star of them all was Dante's *La Vita Nuova*.

La Vita Nuova changed European poetry. Dante was writing not out of traditional convention but fresh from life. The prose he wove round his poems was both storytelling and critical exegesis. He had already written the poems and was thinking back to explain the thoughts and feelings which went into them, events which provoked them and poetic techniques he used. The story of how he came to write the poems became part of the over-arching story: his love for Beatrice. In 1295, Dante was stepping closer to the reader in two revolutionary ways. He was writing his own experience, and doing it not in Latin but vernacular Italian, the language his readers spoke. 'I was afraid to enter it,' he says. 'I remained for several days desiring to write and afraid to begin.'

The story I had to tell was how migration shaped, and carries on re-shaping, the world. I wrote the poems, then added prose to set them in context. The prose interludes are not essays but introductions to each run of poems – as in a live reading poets introduce poems with a little information, so the audience knows something about them when they listen.

<hr>

Like most people I have both migration and rootedness in my background. On my mother's side my family is middle-class professional England, doctors, teachers, potters and scientists. But my father's grandfather, Christian Padel, was born in a German community in Christiansfeld, a border area between Germany and Denmark constantly tugged between these two countries. The town was founded, and a pharmacist's garden was laid out there, in the late eighteenth century by Moravian Brethren, Protestant refugees to Silesia from Moravia in the late seventeenth century. Christian's grandfather Abraham, an apothecary born in Danzig, migrated there to manage the dispensary.

Young Christian went to England for a year or so when he was seven to stay with an uncle who taught music in Harrogate and York. At sixteen he went to Germany to study piano at the Leipzig Conservatoire with the Bohemian virtuoso Ignaz Moscheles, a pupil of Beethoven. In 1865 he travelled to London, and eventually took over his uncle's teaching in York, where he taught the composer George Butterworth and became soloist with the York Symphony Orchestra. When he retired he lived with his son, my grandfather, in Carlisle.

Somewhere, very young, I got the idea that the Padels were Wendish. The Wends or Sorbs are a group of Slavic tribes who have lived in eastern central Germany for over a thousand years, an area which stretches across the River Oder into modern Poland. They kept their language despite pressure to assimilate and persecution under the Third Reich.

As a child, I thought the Wends were nomadic. I pictured them as Gypsies: apothecaries wending their way with piebald ponies and violins through dark forests and open hills, while healing people and playing wild music.

In fact they are mainly farmers not nomads, and whether we really are Wends is not certain. The name Padel is not German, though there are many Padels in eastern Germany and my family's immediate roots are German: they spoke German, not

Danish, in Christiansfeld. But the country with by far the largest number of households called Padel is France, mostly northern France, and the Padels may well have been French Huguenots, which means another earlier migration, escaping Catholic persecution. My branch of Padels migrated from Schleswig, but with me, as with many people, talk of roots and 'Where are you from?' leads to questions, not answers.

London is immigrant city. When the Romans got here in AD 43, they built a settlement on a crossing on the Thames. A hundred thousand indigenous people, the Iceni, burned it down, but the Romans crushed the Iceni and enlarged their trading post into a city. London's walls were built by foreign soldiers, mostly mercenaries from Africa and Spain. Nearly a thousand years later, the Normans invaded: French craftsmen and architects built the Tower of London and Westminster Abbey, the city's oldest landmarks. Like Byzantium, Rome, the Mughal Empire and America, London was created by migration.

We all descend from primeval slime. No one knows how the first cell arrived on Earth, but once it did, whether it was created by a deep-sea biochemical accident or blown in from outer space like the aliens in John Wyndham's fantasy *The Kraken Wakes*, the cell changed everything.

The first type of cell was the prokaryote, a single cell enclosing a circular strand of DNA, which contains the genes. The second type, which makes up most of the life we see every day, plants and animals, was the eukaryotic cell. Its DNA is balled up in a nucleus, tight-packed like the inside of a laptop with different structures called organelles. Each type of organelle has a different function and is enclosed by a membrane.

This was a great improvement on the first design. The membranes, soft inner boundaries, demarcate the organelles and, as in a society, it is their relationships and teamwork which create what life needs – energy. The eukaryote is a house of many chambers and ushered in a new era of life.

For a cell to spread it has to multiply, to copy itself. It breaks apart its DNA so the genetic information can be copied. The prime mover in this is the nucleotide Adenosine triphosphate, the coiner of energy which presides over the whole court of the cell. It begins the drama of replication by snapping the molecule down its long axis. The twirls of the helix unwind into two caterpillar-like halves whose flailing legs are the vulnerable genetic code. Each strand of the parent chromosome acts as a template to create for each flailing leg a new complementary strand, generating a new partner.

So the genetic code is passed on. But the two strands do it differently. The lead strand gives out its code continuously. The other, the lagging strand, grows in the opposite direction, against movement to the replication fork where generation takes place. At the tiniest, most intimate level, it seems, contrariness is built into us. The enzymes that synthesise new DNA can only work in one direction along the parent molecule, so on the lagging strand new DNA is copied in instalments.

Both strands, however, split apart and successfully unite

with new-generated partners, and this is the process which enables living cells to replicate and multiply across the earth. The spread of life depends on this soap opera of relationships, breaking bonds and creating new ones with a swift, enormous violence which is happening inside the cell all the time.

Recently, after the funeral of one of my uncles, I drove to a family gathering at his home in the Chiltern Hills. Near the house I saw a red kite close up. There was a flash of hooded amber eyes and then it swooped away. Its shadow crossed a sunlit field while the bird itself was soaring into blue sky. Suddenly, cells got muddled up in my mind with what they sound like – souls.

For millennia we have taken birds as an image of the soul. Death, we have told each other, is the soul doing what birds do, winging its way to a better place, possibly to return. In sorrow for my uncle, I thought of transmigration: souls migrating into new life, either into a new body or into heaven.

The bird, I thought, and the shadow of the bird. The cell and the soul. Those are the boundaries of migration.

First Cell

Born in a deep-sea vent, synthesised
by lightning in a reducing atmosphere
or carried here by meteorite, we're all
from somewhere else. Algae, first
self-replicating molecule on Earth,

pulls carbon from organic substrate,
performs the world's first magic,
photosynthesis of air to oxygen,
and creates copies of herself, uncountable
as starlings flocking or the pure gold bricks

Sheba sent to Solomon by mule.
Cell in the air, on the rocks. Song
hoping to be heard in a heart cut open.
Little Blue-Green, dreaming of pattern
and form. Tiny horseman of apocalypse.

Dance of the Prokaryotes

Archaea, spirochaete. Cyanobacteria
patterning the genes in a circular
chromosome, like the ring of hippos

dancing in pink tutus in *Fantasia*,
genetic code exposed
on the outside of their home.

Revelation

'A ladder,' the master whispered, 'of nucleic acid.'
This was the first we'd heard of it.
Rain nosed the glass, wind lashed the trees
outside. 'Four hydrogen-bonded nucleotides
locking on like mating damsel flies. But each
a different size, pulling the ladder's sides
into a twist, like serpents on the sign
outside a chemist who for old time's sake
gives lodging in his window to the alchemist's
glass jars.' He drew those twinned snakes
looping up the wand
of God-Who-Escorts-Our-Morphia-Laden-Dead
to forest mist and shadowlands where they belong
and brings them back in dreams.
'But one snake, the lagging strand,
is upside down.' A squeak of chalk.
The pavilion, I recall, was dark.
Rain pooled on the *mesua* floor.
'We're conflict from the start. One thread
runs easy, the other's fitful. Tickertape
on which genetic script, your soul's barcode,
emerges opposite.' What did we know?
We longed for a match, a cellphone, anything
that glowed. 'As in a mirror, messages
are written here and must be read
backwards.' We waited for the prayer

that never came. 'Otherwise is built in.
Behold your molecule of heredity.
Two cosmic serpents, yes; but tail to head.'

Breaking the Bond

Cell summons her treasurer,
hoarder of energy, Adenosine
triphosphate, to break the welded rungs
and separate the partners
in their hydrogen-bond pavane.

Got to be done. Like snapping a bone
to reset it. Now helicase joins the party,
zooming through the knuckled spine
of nucleic acid, tickling the origin-buds
of replication. Don't laugh: she tugs apart

the annealed strands like spiral fronds
of honeysuckle whose soft stems,
sheltering the nest of robins
you watched hatch out last spring,
have grown together, hardening into wood

for years. Helicase spins that poor DNA
like a turbo. Splitting begins,
then copying . . . Replication forks appear
just where you'd say they never could
in the filofax of the nucleus. Its very heart.

Go and Stay

From the kitchen window I see five goldfinches, flakes of flying red and gold flitting through apple boughs above the feeders. They are waiting for the starlings to leave. They raised a family round here this summer: I have watched the chicks grow the scarlet on their faces.

We are lucky to have trees – and very lucky to have goldfinches – in London. London has a whale at the moment too: divers from Marine Life Rescue have seen one in the Thames. They think it is a minke. There are many minke off Scotland, especially around Mull. They must be moving south now for winter.

A cell makes protein, dismantles it and starts again. That is metabolism, which creates the energy cells need in order to respond to whatever is around them. The first metabolising cells emerged from water and set off into the unknown on the adventure of self-replication as if they had heard God say on the fifth day of creation, Go *forth and multiply*. This was the original migration – the spread of blue-green algae over the globe.

Social studies say human migrants are changed by the new home, the place to which they come, but also change that place. This is exactly what the first cells did to earth's atmosphere. They oxygenated it, earth changed and as a result, more complex life forms evolved and spread further.

Five hundred million years ago, proper land plants developed and spread away from the water. A hundred and thirty million years after that the first tree, *Archaeopteris*, developed out of them. It grew sixty to ninety feet high and was the first plant to have large spreading roots. *Archaeopteris* is extinct now but in the late Devonian era, about 370 million years ago, it spread across the world to create the life form which made possible our life on earth – the first forests.

Archaeopteris changed the chemistry of the soil and the atmosphere. Its roots dug in and its ferny canopy absorbed carbon dioxide. Smaller plants developed, taking more carbon dioxide out of the atmosphere while injecting oxygen in. Carbon dioxide levels sank, land temperatures dropped and animals could move over land without overheating because with less carbon dioxide, the ozone layer above earth grew and shielded them from ultraviolet radiation. Trees nourished life in water too, because decaying trunks and leaf litter fed the streams. Freshwater fish evolved. Safe from ultraviolet rays, in a milder climate, the new animals ate food provided by the plants or by each other. Grass evolved and new animals evolved to eat it.

Plant migration made earth a place where animals could breathe. Trees and plants are rooted, but their migration created the forests: their very existence is a result of movement. Cells migrate in the body but stay safely (otherwise we'd all be in trouble) inside it. Migration is part of the restless, constantly self-renewing nature of all life, in creative tension between the fixed and the wandering.

When the starlings fly off, the goldfinches flutter onto the nyger seeds and a blackbird shrills an alarm call from the ancient plum tree.

Our plums are damsons, unusually sweet this year, unusually thick on the bough. Once handled, they change colour for ever: the indigo sheen disappears and you see pink-violet beneath. The tree itself now is almost blue; the plums have pulled the branches low over the grass. My daughter is in London at the moment, working as an intern at a foundation that helps asylum-seekers. She collects the blue plums in a yellow bucket.

Trees seem such fixtures, but they were the first great land migrants. Like their ancestor *Archaeopteris*, modern trees spread over the planet but as the climate changed, ice appeared and trees migrated away from it. Where there was space, as in North America, trees migrated over mountains and crossed continents. Northern trees migrated south during the Pleistocene age (2,600,000 to 11,700 years ago), when the Laurentide Ice Sheet covered North America east of the Rockies from the Arctic down to where New York, St Louis and Kansas City are now. When the world warmed up again, tundra plants recolonised the newly bared soil; then northern trees came back on the fringe of the melting ice. Eighteen thousand years ago came spruce and northern pine; several thousand years afterwards came fir and birch.

But in Britain trees had nowhere to escape to and the last ice age wiped them out, except the strawberry tree in south Ireland. When the ice melted, thirty-three species migrated back to Britain from what is now mainland Europe. First the birch and Scots pine, lastly the hornbeam and beech. Then rising sea levels cut Britain off from Europe, the Channel ended tree migration and Britain was left with those thirty-three, now called our 'native' trees.

But what does 'native' mean? These were post-glacial migrants. The DNA of our most ancient oaks says they came from the Iberian peninsula. That makes the Royal Oak, emblem of England, an immigrant from Spain.

————

Our small garden is stuffed with plants. We have been here fifteen years; my daughter has grown up here as the garden grew shaggier and more jungly. But few of these plants are native. Rhododendrons came from the Himalayas. The damson, like the horse chestnut, came with the Romans – who clearly adored damsons: archaeologists find the stones when digging up Roman camps. The Romans discovered damsons a hundred years before they colonised Britain while conquering a much older civilisation, Syria. But though the damson was first cultivated in Damascus, the oldest continuously inhabited city in the world, wild damsons go back much further. They evolved where the ancestors of apples began too, in south China.

The apple family, *Malus*, probably evolved about twelve million years ago in the mountain system known as Tien Shan, bordering Kazakhstan and Kyrgyzstan. As these mountains rose, the snow melt created subterranean caves and the bear population increased. Through millennia, munching and choosing, extending their territory, bears gradually converted the hawthorn berry into the apple, and the sloe into the damson. They also spread them. Fruit trees migrate by forced migration: the seeds travel in the intestines of animals who drop them, fertilised by dung, in alien soil.

When humans appeared, they spread fruit trees further. They found they could store apples through winter and carry them on journeys. The story of the apple is the story of interaction between plants, animals and people whose horses trod pips into the soil of forests and plains.

Inside all these bears, apples, horses and humans, other life forms were evolving and migrating with them. Four billion years ago some genes discovered they could spread by tricking other genes into replicating them. Parasites replicate their DNA with the help of – and at the expense of – someone else's. They existed long before land animals appeared; new ones evolved at every new stage of life's complexity. Flatworms made their way into crustaceans, then diversified into flukes and tapeworms.

Parasites drove evolution. When their hosts evolved ways of

protecting themselves, parasites adapted to evade the policing and the host had to adapt further to protect itself. The parasites which survived were those that spread into more and better places to live. Today parasites make up most life on earth and outnumber other living species by four to one. Diseases migrated with their hosts.

From a parasite's point of view, many symptoms of disease, like coughing, are the clever ways it has found to change our body's behaviour so that it, itself, may multiply and spread. They do this in thousands of different ways, like the open sores of syphilis, which seems to be a comparatively new disease. Syphilis has always been seen as the unwelcome immigrant, coming from somebody and somewhere else. France called it the Italian Disease, the Dutch the Spanish Disease, Russians called it the Polish Disease, Turks the Christian or Frank Disease, Tahiti the British Disease. It was spread mainly by sailors but no one knows where it began. Was it a New World disease brought to Europe by Colombus or were Hippocratic doctors already describing it in the fourth century BC? The first well-recorded European outbreak was in 1494 among French troops who may have caught it via Spanish mercenaries while besieging Naples. Then it rampaged across Europe. Before 1530 the Italians, Poles and Germans were already calling it the French Disease.

Malaria, though, is much older. As the Romans brought damsons to Britain so humans brought malaria out of Africa. China and ancient Egypt knew it 5,000 years ago, India 3,000 years ago, the Mediterranean 2,500 years ago. Human migration spread it to southern Europe, the Arabian peninsula, Asia, northern Europe. In the fifteenth century, trade and colonisation spread it to the New World and South East Asia through Europe but also via African slaves brought by Spanish colonisers.

Plasmodium, the parasite that causes malaria, is passed on by the female anopheline mosquito which needs blood to develop her eggs. (Only the females bite; males stick to glucose.) The parasite develops in her tiny gut, enters our blood through her saliva and is carried into the liver where it invades cells and multiplies. Then it returns to the blood, penetrates red cells and multiplies further, breaking down the red cells.

Today a million and a half people die from malaria every year. *Plasmodium*, like computer hackers, always tries to be ahead of the game: it is constantly developing immunity to chemicals we find to counter it. Every forty-five seconds, says an ad in my newspaper today, another child dies of malaria. Nature's forms do not demonstrate benevolence, said Darwin, divine or otherwise.

In Christianity, the Fall is the story of how something harmful got into the system from the start. One name for Satan is *alienus*, the stranger, the outsider. Parasites tell the same story: cells have smaller cells within them that flourish at their expense and accompany them everywhere. We, mosquitoes and *Plasmodium* evolved and spread together.

***

But though migration spreads disease, migration also defends us from it. Atoms migrate in a molecule, teeth migrate in our mouths and cells migrate in our bodies. They move by pushing protrusions out at their front and drawing in their trailing ends. Their migration is the Go-and-Stay type and happens for two reasons.

One is to create new life: cells migrate in a pregnant mother to form a foetus. The other is to defend us against harm. Cell migration is the basis of the immune system. Cells migrate to a site of infection or trauma, travelling towards wounds to attack invading bacteria.

Cells migrate, in other words, to heal, repair damage and create new life. This is not circulation, but the maintenance of our fabric.

'Cells are guided,' a cell biologist told me, 'by migration-promoting chemicals they detect in their environment. They find some attractive and like to go towards them, they find others repulsive and try to get away from them. If you supply the chemical with a needle and move your needle around, the cells chase it.'

'Why call it migrating?' I asked.

'To give an impression of purpose,' he said. 'The cells just seem to be trying to go somewhere. Purposefully.'

So, I wondered, is all motivation ultimately chemical? Maybe the answer is that all purpose has some chemical dimension, but – as with the different factors of push and pull behind human and animal migration – that doesn't mean there aren't others, too. Our own bodies show us that however many purposes there are behind migration, two are constant – to heal and to create new life.

Allele

The variant. Scripture from a chamber of errors.
The ghost who stalks the body like a shadow
in the mirror, invisible – just so –

as planktonic stars on pulsing gills of foam
that seem themselves an animal
in the wake of the midnight ferry.

The Other, who reveals where you'll go
next. The stranger who should be welcome
in your home, for *stranger* may also be *god*.

Cell Begins Her Travels

Cytoskeleton, little net
of peel and fibrous scaffolding
within the cytoplasm, protects
Cell's shape so Cell can move, repair
the wound, attack a virus, create
an embryo. Cell waves longhaired
flagella like the spray of spores on mould.
In a blitz of lamellipodia, Cell
sprouts her motile fronds. She, the queen bee,
will fibrillate each organelle
in turn. Her ruffling front slides on,
retracts, moves on again.
So Cell migrates
like an old soul bent on heaven.

Spinning the Plasma

Nurse presses the switch
on the Refletron Blood-measurer
Machine, vulnerable
to rotor fatigue, and squeezes
bead-berries from the tip
of this stringy boy's index finger.

He sits sweat-sheathed
on his mother's knee.
Nurse spins the plastic wheel
like prayer, like fortune, till
hay-colour liquid separates from dark
sediment in red cells.

They have been penetrated
by *Plasmodium falciparum.*
The parasite has multiplied,
breaking the red cells down
which spells fever, shivering,
fever again
until – in the uncertain mill

of evolution
all hardworking parasites pursue,
shape-shifting to hoodies and hackers

as attempts to outwit them change –
it's curtains. Yes. Their mass
obstructs blood vessels in his brain.

Flight of the Apple

(for Barrie Juniper)

Fly me beyond Taklamakan Desert
and the blossom trees of immortality
to heaven's mountain Tien Shan,
heaving itself into air above the snowline.
Melt pours down. Floods
carve an underworld of caves
and in move the bears, whose lazy sorcery
turns hawthorn bullets into quince
and apple. Because everyone, given time,
changes everyone else. It's a world on fire
and the horse falls in love, the wild red
long-maned horse of the Lascaux Cave

whose teeth and gut help this pip
on its adventure. Hooves
drive the apple core deep
in the soil of the steppe
and the Turkic corridor. Horse dung
and dung beetle spread invisible
orchards, wouldn't you know,
hidden in the heart of apple – to William Tell
protesting an unjust edict,
Newton dozing in a Cambridge garden,
to Eden, to Eve. So apples sprang
wherever we tamed the horse.

Go *and* Come Back

The mornings are dark now, it is late October, the clocks have gone back like the songbirds, leaves are falling and the kitchen radio is saying they have found that whale dead in the Thames near Dartford. He was a young male with a totally empty stomach. He probably starved to death. But he's not a minke, he's a humpback. Humpbacks are occasionally seen off the west coast of Scotland but it's amazing to have one in the Thames. He should have been making his way slowly from the Arctic to the tropics but like all young males he was curious. It could have been his first lone exploration and it went wrong. Migration can be very wasteful.

Animals travel in many different ways through different environments all the time and there seems to be no definition accepted by every zoologist that covers all their migrations. Some are classic there-and-back affairs like the humpbacks from Arctic to tropics, or monarch butterflies between Alaska and Mexico, which happen at a specific season or particular moment in the creature's life cycle. Others are journeys from which the adults never return, only the children.

Migrations are thousands of miles and take months; migrations are a few miles and take less than an hour. They are seasonal and daily, regular and once-in-a-lifetime. Some are predictable, some seem quite random. Some are done by a group, others by lone individuals. Some creatures make epic journeys just to feed their young, like the albatross which flies for hours out to sea to bring back food for its helpless, land-locked chick. The dispersing young of many species migrate away from their parents' territories to find their own. Some animals seem pure nomads, constantly shifting in response to food and weather. Kangaroos follow no pattern in ranging through the Australian bush – is that migration? There are daily migrations like human commutes, regular migrations and once-only journeys. Some are predictable as clockwork, others seem entirely random – or so fluid that the animals seem to be responding to the slightest shift in wind.

Even seasonal migrations happen for different reasons. Many go to escape winter weather but the yellow-lipped sea kraits of the South Pacific migrate to a safe place to shed their skin, always a vulnerable moment, and tens of thousands of shelduck leave Britain and northern Europe after breeding to moult in one place – the Waddensee, mudflats off the coast of north Germany.

Male sperm whales, Australian giant cuttlefish and diamond pythons migrate to mate, setting off on arduous journeys in search of a female. Others, like grey whales, green turtles and emperor penguins, migrate to lay eggs or give birth in safety.

Some creatures migrate to find an essential mineral. But mostly it is for food. Everyone wants the best for their children: parents need food to get the energy to find more food for the babies. Swifts come to Britain to raise families because in summer there are fewer birds competing for the high-flying insects they eat than in tropical Africa, and longer daylight hours to find them in. North American migrant birds who winter in Mexico raise their young in the northern forests of Canada for the same reason.

The tropics offer plentiful insects and seeds and it's always warm, but the duration of daylight never increases and there is not enough food for everyone. So migrants raise their young where there's the best chance of getting food, leave when it disappears and return when it comes back. Temperatures change with the seasons, plants bear fruit at different times and when food fails, animals go to where it is. In summer the Arctic has extraordinarily rich, concentrated insect life in the air and plankton in the sea: thousands of birds and marine creatures go there to eat and breed. But to survive there in winter they would have to change physically and compete with other life forms through months when there's practically no food at all. So, from whales to warblers, they evolved to migrate.

Bird migration is the heartbeat of the planet. Along ancient routes, nothing to do with human frontiers, millions of birds are weaving the world together all the time. They are migration's blueprint, reminding us that both earth and the life it sustains are constantly changing form and changing place. It is especially their migrations which have made birds, for us, an image of hope.

'Hopes are shy birds,' wrote John James Audubon in his journal in 1820, 'flying at a great distance.' Audubon had been fascinated by birds since he was young. He had just said goodbye to his beloved wife and children and was taking a boat down the Ohio river on the first leg of his journey to Britain, where he hoped to find someone to print and publish his bird paintings. There, giving a talk in Edinburgh on the birds of North America, he would inspire a sixteen-year-old medical student (called 'Bobby' by his family) who hated the course he was doing just as Audubon had once hated being a naval cadet.

Audubon and that reluctant medical student had a couple of things in common. Both had to cope with great loss when they were small and did it by turning to nature – to long solitary walks and birdwatching. Audubon chose birds (or they chose him) as a way to make sense of the world. His mother died when he was little. Charles Darwin's died when he was eight. 'Why does every gentleman not become an ornithologist?' Darwin wondered when he was ten. At Edinburgh, instead of attending operations and medical lectures, Darwin took bird-stuffing tutorials from a local taxidermist. Birds are an image of escape from where and what you are right now. 'Hope is the thing with feathers,' says Emily Dickinson, 'That perches in the soul.'

Audubon was born in 1785, twenty-four years before Darwin, on Haiti, then a French colony called Saint-Domingue whose sugar and indigo plantations, worked by African slaves, supplied two-thirds of France's overseas trade. He was the illegitimate child of a Creole chambermaid from Louisiana and a French naval officer who owned a plantation and sold it before the slave rebellions began in 1791. When his mother died, Audubon's father took him to France, formally adopted him and brought him up in Nantes through the turmoil of the French Revolution. He grew up roaming the woods, bringing home birds' eggs and nests to draw. His father encouraged him, pointing out birds' movements, their sense of danger, their seasonal comings and goings.

But his father also wanted his son to be a sailor like himself and sent him, aged twelve, to military school. Audubon hated it, failed his officer's qualifications and went back to exploring the woods. In 1803 his father procured him a false passport and to prevent him from being conscripted into Napoleon's army sent him to America, to a farm bought with the plantation money on Perkiomen Creek, Philadelphia.

Here, Audubon continued to study birds. One of his experiments was to tie strings to the legs of eastern phoebes and prove that they returned to the same nesting sites each year. This was the first known bird-banding experiment in America. It is no accident, perhaps, that the young man who proved that birds came back to their first homes was a double immigrant who had already lost two homes of his own. Birds leave but come back, like the dove to Noah. Birds are images of escape but also of return.

It was escape which drove Daedalus, the mythical sculptor and inventor imprisoned on the island of Crete, to imitate birds and make wings for himself and his son Icarus, who, on their migration, flew too near the sun and fell into the sea. And it was escape that gave a name, the Wild Geese, to thousands of Catholic Irishmen who left Ireland to serve King James in France when English Protestants had beaten his army.

Caged or free, birds say it all. 'Oh that I had wings like a dove,' says Psalm 55. 'I would fly away and be at rest.' 'A robin redbreast in a cage,' William Blake said at a time when people still did cage robins in Britain, 'puts all of Heaven in a rage.' In Dickens's *Bleak House*, the poignantly named Miss Flyte, unhinged by the delays of her lawsuit, keeps wild birds in cages which she will open when her case is heard. The list of their names, charting what she and others have lost because of these delays, begins with Hope, goes on with Joy and Youth and ends with the injustices she cannot fly from: Waste, Want, Ruin, Despair, Madness.

We compare ourselves with nature and see ourselves reflected in it. Migration seems to lie at the heart of the birds' mystery; we feel they are free, as we long to be free, to get away – and, if they want, to come back.

Through the ages we have believed that along with the freedom to fly, birds have special powers, special knowledge and a special language. In ancient Greece and Rome, augurs deciphered their flight and their calls. Birds were omens, birds were the gods' messengers. The canary down the mine whose death warns miners of gas, like the dove with a green twig which tells Noah the Flood is subsiding, belong with an ancient feeling that birds are sign-bearers and foretell the future. 'Take note when you hear the voice of the cranes,' says the Greek poet Hesiod in the seventh century BC. 'Every year they call from the clouds above. They give the signal for ploughing, they mark the season of rainy winter.' Birds go between two worlds, and between air and earth, so why not between us and the gods?

Mediaeval alchemists spoke of a mystical 'Language of Birds' which translated what was divine, therefore of the air, into the base earth of humanity. Birds speak to us of distance; as in a poem by Matsuo Bashō, written as he travelled to the wild interior of seventeenth-century Japan:

> The horse turns his head –
> from across the distant plain
> a cuckoo calling.

Birds are harbingers of change. Maybe dangerous change like a storm or a battle – Homer compares the sound of the advancing Trojan army to cries of migrating cranes – but often hopeful change, like spring. To those who stay home, the great thing migrants say is renewal. Ancient Greek children welcomed swallows as messengers of spring in their traditional 'swallow songs'. 'They've made it again,' says Ted Hughes of swifts in *Season Songs*, 'which means the globe's still working.'

In Bhutan, where black-necked cranes are vital characters in folksong and folklore, the magic moment is late October when these birds wing in from Ladakh and Tibet. They come to just two places. I visited one, a bleak yellow marsh called Phobjikha, while looking for Bhutan's tigers. It was late March, the cranes had just left and everyone was feeling desolate. In October the villagers and the whole country wait anxiously for them to come back. If they're late it may mean bad luck or a ferocious winter, so their arrival is a national event. In November, when they are safely back, thousands of people celebrate the black-necked crane Festival.

Bird migration has sometimes been a bit too mysterious to get our heads around. The Greeks and the Old Testament prophets took it for granted. 'The stork in the heaven knoweth her appointed times,' says Jeremiah, 'the turtle, the crane and the swallow observe the time of their coming.' But in the Middle Ages this knowledge disappeared, as if mediaeval man couldn't believe that birds crossed the oceans he found so dangerous. 'Migrate' was first used in English (or rather first recorded) of people. That was 1611; it was used in 1646 of animals and only in 1697 did it begin to be used of birds. Where did swallows go in winter? It was commonly agreed (maybe swallows taking wet mud to make their nests helped the idea along) that they hibernated at the bottom of rivers. Mediaeval drawings even show fishermen netting swallows along with their fish.

Even Dr Johnson, in the eighteenth century, believed this. Bird migration is one of the wonders of the world and the theories we have come up with to explain it show how extraordinary it is. Aristotle knew swallows went to Africa for winter. He also noticed that different birds used the same habitat at different times of year. He saw redstarts in summer, he says, where in winter he saw robins. Early translators of his work knew less about bird migration than he did and translated him wrong. In their versions, Aristotle seemed to be saying that redstarts changed to robins in the winter. Only in the eighteenth century did someone test this theory by keeping redstarts throughout the year.

Above my head come the ancient cries of geese on a journey. Their asymmetrical V slides across the white sky like the long black tick to a maths problem. This winter Britain will get about sixty species of autumn migrant from Scandinavia and northern Europe where their food is disappearing under ice. They are mainly large water birds, but also some of the thrush family, and others who winter here but nest in the southern hemisphere.

Since the Middle Ages we have uncovered various bird migrating secrets. We know where many go, partly from bird-ringing or bird-banding. You catch the bird gently, put a light band on its leg saying where and when you saw it, and if it's caught again somewhere else you have its route, or at least the two end points.

Radar helps, too. A flock of migrating songbirds shows up on radar as clusters of moving green dots. Radar was originally developed to track aircraft and was key to Britain's success in the Battle of Britain. Pilots saw mysterious moving objects that were not other aircraft and called them 'angels'. Later they realised their radar angels were migrating birds. After the war, scientists used radar to map migrations and discovered a complex global knitting pattern of flyways. We now know that nearly a fifth of the world's ten thousand bird species are long-distance migrants. In the southern hemisphere birds breed in the south and migrate north for winter, but because there is less land in the far south to support life, most bird migration happens in the Northern Hemisphere.

The geese above our garden breed in the north and go south for winter like many other species: millions of brilliantly coloured American warblers, for instance, or Europe's smallest seabird, the European storm petrel.

Petrels skim the waves, sipping planktonic food from the surface and seeming to pat the water with first one trailing foot then the other. Sailors called them *peterelles*, 'Little St Peters', after the Apostle who walked on water. They thought storm petrels were an omen of bad weather and called them the children of storm.

When autumn temperatures drop, storm petrels leave the cliff where they raise their single chick – say, on the rocky remote island of Little Skellig in Southern Ireland – and fly to South Africa. They return in April, a thirteen-thousand mile-round trip, arriving after sunset to avoid getting attacked by gulls. One was once ringed on Little Skellig, set free and caught again thirteen years later. The delighted birders gave her a new ring and let her loose. That bird, so small it would fit inside your hand, had flown between South Africa and Kerry at least twenty-six times.

Many birds follow coasts, mountain ranges and river valleys. This works well in North America where coasts, mountain chains and large rivers run mainly north to south and where the four great flyways are the Atlantic coast, the Mississippi, the centre of the country and up the Pacific. (For most birds that fly on into South America these routes merge into one over Panama.) But between Europe and Africa, and over Asia, things are more complicated because the big barriers, the Alps and Himalayas, run east-west. So does that other barrier, the Mediterranean Sea.

Large land birds like storks and eagles rise on thermals of warm air and have to cross a sea in one long glide, because thermals do not form over sea. They look for the same routes human migrants try to find: the shortest crossing like the Straits of Gibraltar, western link between Europe and Africa, or the Dardanelles, eastern link between Europe and Asia.

When my daughter finished university we went to Istanbul and Troy. One September afternoon we looked up from walls built when the city was still called Byzantium and saw storks flying overhead from the Danube Delta to Africa, as they have done before Byzantium and Troy were founded. In spring, the skies above Israel too fill with storks flying north from Africa to nest in Poland, France and Germany.

Sea birds, mainly smaller than storks and eagles, don't need to worry about falling into oceans and it is they that migrate furthest. Some migrate in long loops. Wilson's storm petrels fly figures of eight from Antarctic breeding grounds to sub-Arctic feeding grounds and back; sooty shearwaters fly a different figure of eight across the Pacific from New Zealand and back, a round trip of forty thousand miles; Matsudaira's storm petrel flies East-West between the Indian and Pacific Oceans. One record-breaking Manx shearwater is known to have clocked up five million miles in its fifty-something years. The little grey-mantled arctic tern flies from its nest at the North Pole to the South Pole and back, a round trip of 45,000 miles. It eats and sleeps on the wing. During that time it never touches land and hardly uses its feet at all. A young one, ringed as a chick on the Farne Islands off Britain's east coast, once reached Melbourne three months after it fledged – a maiden journey of 4,000 miles.

But migration is as various as physiology. Both in little countries like Britain and huge countries like India there are internal migrations in winter, when birds shift from the country to a city or from north to south. Some birds simply go up and down the same mountain all their life. Nepal's national bird, the beautiful monal pheasant, migrates vertically between 2,000 and 4,000 metres, down when snow is thick and up when it melts.

<hr />

Behind all this activity are two physical facts, the spinning and the tilt of the earth. As the angled globe rotates, temperatures drop variably in different places so birds move towards food and warmth.

Nesting, which means breeding, is the key. Nesting seems the opposite of migration but is also its goal. These geese will go back north in spring to raise a new family while summer migrants like swifts and warblers come from the Mediterranean and Africa to do the same thing here.

Go-and-Come-Back migration evolved as animals and birds adapted to terrain that was difficult to live in for part of the year and even, for some species, part of the day. It is a response to changes in the surrounding world outside and its evolutionary point is survival.

Their journeys and routes, their reasons for migrating, the risks they face and strategies they come up with, are parables for human migration too. How could birds not be our symbol of hope?

Dunlin

Light bursts around the body. . . Moving on
to wetland beyond full moon, next
water-and-feed. Draw breath; ease
hot muscle-protein, catabolised
in every dwindling breast.

Then the V, and my wing pushes down
making upwash off the tip
which my neighbour taps
and gets his lift for free.
Energy, flock, energy is everything.

Windflow, moonshadow. We read
the ground below. The rocking dark
protects. Over desert, not to overheat,
we take rock cover through the day.
In air we keep in touch, calling.

Insects, estuary, rest. Take off again
like that torn carob leaf
floating from shallow to open sea
beyond the headland, poised between
its own reflection and the white-spun meridian.

Where Clavicle and Wishbone Fuse

Radar operators, picking up echoes from migrating birds
write 'Angels' in the logbook, because they come

unbidden. Their licking silhouettes belong
to the school of night, drawn on

for hours across the moon by a magnetism you might
if they were us, call faith, and they keep going

on a butterball of gold fat glowing
in the breast like a secret love

where clavicle and wishbone fuse.
Silk-gristle wings, so easily blown off-course

or bagged by hawks and guns
in blue-blush-ivory dawn

at crossing-points of continents: Bosphorus,
Camargue, Gibraltar. Triggered by high winds,

barometric pressure, a drop in temperature,
the dying of summer flies or autumn seed; and inner
                                                    need.

Children of Storm

(for Jeremy Mynott)

This is Skellig Michael, off the coast
of Kerry, darksummer home
to guillemots, shearwaters
and the bad-luck good-luck guys –
St Peter's Birds, the outriders,
who lay their one and only egg
in a chink of wall
which they enter and leave at night.
Yes it's touch and go
for Mother Carey's Chickens
hunting microscopic prey
with dangling toes as if they walked
over whipped-and-peaking waves.
They gather in charcoal twilight
flashing silver question marks
under black-sickle wings
then take off for the Cape
from this millefeuille granite ledge
over creamy North Atlantic thunderheads
to Africa's cliffs of lemon cloisonné,
sand schist. It would make a dog think
to see the same five grams
of close-feather muscle
venting back to where they hatched –
black igloo churches

growing on black rock like its own flesh,
recorded in the Martyrology of Tallaght
and Annals of Innisfallen.
Come spring, the Priest's Stone
watches for them at sunset
against a shine-and-shadowboxing sea.

Swallows Hibernating at the Bottom of a River

– and a fisherman pulls them out in his net
along with dancing tench, bream, barbel,

cleft wings trickling, marbled in January sun
by headwater freshets,

the coiled-wire leg bones
you'd never normally see

tucked in riparian mud
like prayers engraved on a rice grain.

Rift

I give you Lotan, heart of Arava Valley
in the Gulf of Aqaba. Turn your head
to the umber-maroon of Jordan's mountains.
Turn again and it's mountains of the Negev
where shell-rock glimmers white as halogen.
If you come this evening, as you surely will come,
what you'll get is the mulberry glow
of a holy sunset, plus six thousand white storks
gliding between Africa and Europe
on warm blue thermals of spring,
scudding out from the cloudrim like rain
over this wound in earth's crust, opened
in the underworld by a clash of tectonic
plates from Turkey to Mozambique.

The Boy from Haiti

(for Mark Cocker)

He's eighteen, escaping conscription,
abandoning France. On the open sea
here's Earth's rim like he's never seen it,
a blurred brush-line of purple on aquamarine.

'Sorrow. Deep melancholy. My affections
still with those I left behind. The world
seemed a great wilderness.' Haiti at three,
the forest at Nantes, and now this.

He can't remember leaving Saint Domingue.
Wherever he's been he's watched birds.
'I felt an intimacy with them, bordering
on frenzy.' He reads La Fontaine

and scatters ship's biscuit on deck.
A flock of migrating pipits falls
from the heavens like a shaft of winter sun.
'They came on board wearied. So hungry.'

The crew see a forest, a shore. . .
He knew it. Birds unlock
everything. An inlet, wide, deep and certain.
Cries of gulls above East River docks.

The Watcher

(for Tim Birkhead)

Midnight in the castle at Radolfzell.
I'm gazing at our pixellated map
    of the Dark Continent
and a luminous full stop: a radio transmitter
fitted in east Germany five months ago
by a Vogelwarte Research Station ringer
to the leg – before wing-feathers grew –
    of a juvenile white stork
now standing in scorched savannah.
The pulsar, monitored by satellite,
flashes at the frequency of my heart.

Outside in the castle orchard, low winter sun
throws shadows longer than the trees.
    Why am I here? To record.
And – oh yes – retrace that juvenile's first journey.
One mouse click and a red vine grows
over eastern Europe, Eilat and Sudan to Chad
tracing the flight of magnetite, lodged between
    white stork skull and white stork brain,
held to Earth's magnetic field over mountains, sea,
fumes from the cities, frontier guns,
a thousand no-man's-lands, a thousand wars.
Not one year old and it's on the double pilgrimage
white storks evolved to make. Click again.

Quest for the sacred. And if I
could track that one stork down
on its winter ground, maybe I'd know
what has become of life and me
and where to go. I'd pour libations, follow
        the omen, set up sacrifice
to the god of wayfarers, even pay a call
on the seer who decodes
the flight of birds. I'd prophesy.

Finding the Way

It is a gold and blue November day. Sun speckles my daughter's blonde hair as she sweeps up dead leaves, geese are still coming over from Scandinavia and I am digging up a bush. A robin, who sees this garden as his (or her) territory, is watching. When I bed the root in new earth it hops down to investigate and we look at each other.

Robins are the essence of a British garden. But the mysteries they hold go right to the heart of migration.

Many birds return to the same cliff or nest as the previous year and only get lost when storms blow them off-course. Young birds with no parental guidance, such as ospreys, end up exactly where their species has always wintered without ever having seen the place or route. A baby cuckoo raised by non-migrating foster parents will never know its real parents, yet migrates south along the routes they use to join other cuckoos in wintering grounds of East Africa and South East Asia. It is not only direction they get right, but timing. In some species, mated pairs spend the winter apart and synchronise their return to reach the nesting site separately within the same few hours.

How do they do it? We who lose our way so easily without satnav marvel that birds reach the right place from so far away.

For both timing and navigation, birds use a whole range of tools, some we share and some we don't. Parental guidance is the most obvious. We can relate to that – we often start our own life-course by following parents. Migrants who have done it before are the best navigators. Geese, like swans and cranes, migrate in family units. There are parents up there guiding their young, taking turns to lead, teaching them to follow the route and recognise landmarks like rivers, coasts, mountains and cities so they form their own mental map.

Young birds must also learn to deal with high winds and storms. Geese can copy parents but ospreys do it alone, and satellite trackings have shown how much better older ospreys are at correcting for wind drift. Young ospreys learn without a tutor, on the job.

Birds also navigate by sound. Sound orientates, helps you know where you are, where you're going and who's going with you: they steer you by waves crashing on the coast, a city's hum, the rustle of a forest, each other's contact calls. Migrating birds don't sing, they need their breath to fly, but those who migrate in groups utter road cries, a sonic hand-holding – *I'm here, are you?* – which keeps them in touch about what's happening and where they're going. The film *Winged Migration* follows a group of geese across Central Europe. The camera flies beside them as their wing muscles beat and contract, and they call constantly to each other as the land rolls away beneath. Migration can be a noisy affair.

Birds steer by smell, too. It may be strange to think of a hard beak picking up scent, but birds have a fantastic sense of smell. They need it to find food. Sea, rivers, mountains, woods and cities, they smell them all.

But senses we share with them are only the beginning of their toolkit. Our senses are not the world, they are only filters set by the limits of human physiology. Birds have an inbuilt sun compass and respond to patterns of polarised light and barometric pressure. Those that fly from pole to pole allow for earth's rotation, and those that migrate at night – when the air is cooler, and dense like dark cream, with less risk of overheating or water loss over desert, less turbulence rising from earth like bad dreams to throw them off-course – are imprinted with a particular map of the stars and steer by a star compass.

Their combination of precise timing and direction is demonstrated by the phenomenon known as *Zugunruhe*, 'journey unease' or 'restlessness about the move'. If a migratory bird is restrained during the hours it would normally migrate, it flutters and agitates for as long as its journey would take, in the to-and-fro twitchery you see in swallows before they go as their bodies are first preparing and then impelling them to fly. If the journey would normally take twelve hours, *Zugunruhe* lasts as long as that. If the species does a five-day journey, *Zugunruhe* lasts five days.

Scientists study *Zugunruhe* in the Emlen Funnel, a cage

shaped like the collar you put on a dog's neck to stop it licking a wound. The bird flutters up in it and slips down again and again. There is an ink pad on the bottom, so on each attempt it leaves an inky trail which points in the precise direction their migration would take. If the lab has a planetarium-like night sky, scientists can change the star pattern and watch the bird change its angle of flutter. How long it tries depends on how many hours, days or months it would normally take to migrate.

Behind a lot of this is a bird's response to earth's magnetic field.

In 1961 a geologist called Heinz Lowenstam made a momentous discovery – that living organisms contained in their bodies the mineral magnetite. Up to this point, everyone assumed that magnetite existed only in inorganic materials. The Greeks called magnetic rock after Magnesia, in Asia Minor, where a lot of it was found. Its power to attract iron was supposedly discovered by the sixth-century BC philosopher Thales (although one myth says it was a shepherd called Magnes) and in English it was known as lodestone: the 'leading' stone. Pilots were lodesmen; the Pole Star which led you north was the lodestar. Until 1961 magnetic rock was a static, inorganic thing which paradoxically caused other inorganic things to move.

Lowenstam was born in 1912 in Upper Silesia, a mining district in south-east Germany which, when Lowenstam was seven, was given to Poland after the First World War. He grew up fascinated by stone, studied geology in Munich and went to Palestine to research the East Nazareth Mountains. He came back to Munich in 1936, a week after a new law had forbidden

Jews to receive doctorates. In 1937 he migrated to America where thirty years later he published a paper announcing that certain sea molluscs known for their homing ability had crystals of iron oxide in the tips of their teeth. Lowenstam suggested that these molluscs were bio-synthesising magnetite and found their way using a magnetic compass. Magnetism, he argued, must be a property of organic as well as inorganic things like stars and stones.

Geologists were sceptical, but in 1975 magnetite was discovered in another life form, magnetotactic bacteria, which swung into line along earth's magnetic field. Bio-mineralism was accepted as a new fact of life.

I love that Lowenstam was a migrant like Audubon. The country he was born into became another nation when he was seven. At thirty-five he emigrated to survive. One immigrant found birds returning to the same nest year after year, the other found that magnetism is a property of living beings.

Thanks to Lowenstam we now know that magnetite plays an important role in the behaviour of a whole range of life forms: from birds to bees, crocodiles, tuna, fungi, sea turtles, fruit flies, sharks and lobsters. The fossil record goes back at least two billion years. Magnetite operates in them as a membrane-bound bio-mineral, helping them navigate by sensitivity to earth's magnetic field.

The advantage of a magnetic compass in your brain, thorax or teeth is that you are not affected by cloud or changes in daylight hours. The disadvantage is that you can be thrown off-course by electric storms or sunspot activity. Birds are disorientated by electric disturbance and get lost; mass beachings of sperm whales suggest that sunspots disable their magnetic compass.

Some species have magnetite in their brain or skull; monarch butterflies have traces in their thorax; pigeons in their upper beak. Some birds who migrate at night have a special light-processing region of the brain called (rather like a new galaxy) Cluster N. If our robin migrates this autumn, Cluster N will let it read the earth's magnetic field through photoreceptor molecules connected to the eye. 'Usually the left,' one of my uncles told me. He is a neuroscientist who works on the brain and eye. 'No one knows why.'

Earth's magnetic field is doughnut-shaped. Its elliptic force-lines run between North and South Poles like bars around a squirrel-proof bird-feeder. It turns out most animals know what part of the earth's surface they are flying, crawling or swimming over, because they detect the changing angles.

But birds, who seem so free, are slaves to their genes. Their precise timings, and the direction they take, are the result of genetic programming: complex inner drives passed down in their DNA. Their bodies and brains order them where to go and when. Because the earth rotates, they might have to fly an extra hundred miles if they are five minutes late in setting out, so a punctilious schedule could make the difference between life and death.

⸻

Migration makes enormous physical demands and birds prepare for it like athletes before a race. Feathers and pectoral muscles are crucial and to get feathers in perfect condition many birds moult before they go.

Heart and breath are crucial, too. A bird's heart is six times bigger than ours in proportion to its weight, and their respiratory systems are even more dramatically different. Ours is 5 per cent of our volume; a bird's is twenty.

But fuel is the key – do you take it with you or find it on the way? How they manage their energy determines their options. Catabolism is the set of pathways that break down molecules into smaller units and release energy. Birds who store up fat before long non-stop flights gradually deplete it and then start catabolising their protein, which they lose variably – from digestive organs and, more dangerously, the all-important breast muscles.

Large birds are already near the limit their wings can bear so they have to stop and feed on the way, but many little birds take their fuel with them like camels. Those who fly four or five days non-stop cram in food beforehand to build up fat. Some search out the kind of hormonal boost athletes find in steroids. Semi-palmated sandpipers fly for three days and nights over open water from the Canadian Arctic to South America. Beforehand the cooler temperatures and shorter days of autumn trigger hormonal changes which make them switch to a high-fat diet. Their gut grows so they can eat more. En route they stop at the Bay of Fundy on Canada's eastern coast to gorge on mud shrimp loaded with Omega-3 fatty acids. Over two weeks their body mass doubles, their muscles use oxygen more efficiently – and off they fly to South America.

Birds that migrate in flocks help each other. In V-formation, the leader breaks up the wall of air, creating a swirl that helps the birds behind, then drops back to let another take over. Everyone flies in the upwash from the wingtip vortex of the bird ahead. V-formation saves crucial energy: birds fly 70 per cent further and often faster than they can alone.

Some birds migrate solo, usually because of diet. Hummingbirds feed off flowers. You can't queue up and wait for a flower to make more nectar so they go alone, though when many are on the move they often travel in parallel flyways like commuters on the motorway.

At the other end of the spectrum is the osprey with its six-foot wingspan. Ospreys eat fish, and fishing too is often most effective alone. They mate for life but spend the winter apart. Most British ospreys winter in West Africa (some from Eastern Europe go as far as South Africa), while male American ospreys who winter in Florida may fly north to Maine to wait for their mates. Of a pair which nests in Scotland, the male arrives from Africa, then the female comes in by her own route. When they go, they leave the chicks, who may never have caught a fish alone, to find their own way.

Some birds follow different routes out and back. One of the greatest animal feats of endurance and navigation is performed every year by the tiny blackpoll warblers. The distance each one flies in its life is the equivalent for us of ten return journeys to the moon but that's nothing compared to the dangers of their autumn migration.

In spring they leave the tropical forests and coffee plantations of Venezuela and Brazil where they winter and fly north
over the Gulf of Mexico, up the Mississippi Valley, over the
Great Plains to Canada and Alaska, where they build little cup
nests in small fir trees. Everything about them is small except
the risk they take going back.

When their three weeks of parenting are over, they eat to
fuel their return. In a few days they double their body mass,
storing fat and protein, swelling their gut. If you held one in
your hand at this point and blew the feathers apart you'd see
bubbles of fat held in by grey, stretched skin.

In September they head south-east over the Great Lakes,
rest on the New England coast and divide. Some follow the
east coast down to Florida and cross the Caribbean, others go
to South Carolina and island-hop through the Bahamas and
West Indies to South America. But some, the risk-takers, fly
east over the Atlantic and pick up strong winds which hurl
them south-west over the east Caribbean, non-stop day and
night, eighty-eight hours to Venezuela. Four days over the sea
at 16,000 feet. Why so high? Maybe to find the best tailwinds.
Or maybe for cooler air, to stop their miniscule breast muscles
overheating.

The reason it is so – well, if they were human we'd say brave
or reckless – is tropical storms. Autumn in the Caribbean is
peak hurricane season. They are swept into spiralling winds,
towering clouds, torrential rain. Many crash exhausted in the
sea, others become disoriented, are sucked into a depression,
hurtle across the Atlantic and land in north-west Europe where
they are lost to their species with no chance of making it back:

prevailing winds over the Atlantic blow east and they are only programmed to fly south.

Nature is prodigal, said Darwin. So much waste.

But migration is about survival and most blackpoll warblers make it. Every speck of fat burns off. But if they survive it's worth it because the hurricane route is shorter by 1,500 miles. They get a head start on establishing a feeding territory in the new home.

<hr />

Another story of waste, risk and endurance shows how ancient the birds' flyways are. Bar-headed geese nest in Central Asia but winter on the other side of the Himalayas in Assam, north Burma and wetlands of Pakistan. They go early before autumn storms and try to do the thousand miles over the mountains in one day. They gather in a valley, check the air pressure, open their charcoal-tipped wings and up they go.

At fifty miles per hour they pick up tailwinds and double their speed. In those winds every millisecond is a fight. If a storm rises and a young one falls out the mother has to keep going. If forced to land on the near-vertical mountainside they sleep in the snow and try again. Some don't wake and the living will freeze too unless they go at once. There's nothing to eat or drink, it's now or never.

The oxygen a bird needs to keep flapping is twenty times what it needs at rest and up here the air has a quarter of the oxygen available at sea level. But their bodies are uniquely adapted to the altitude. Their haemoglobin absorbs oxygen faster than that of any other bird and their capillary veins penetrate unusually deep in to their muscle, so the oxygen reaches further and they get more from each breath. They are powerful flapping machines and their circulation keeps their wings so warm that the roof-air of the planet cannot stipple them with ice.

Why are they like this, able to fly over Everest? Because they and their route are older than the Himalayas. Over the millennia, as these rocks rose across their path, they adapted their physiology to the increasing altitude. Their destiny is written in their genes. They went where their DNA said and instead of finding a way around they adapted to the increasingly demanding conditions. And year after year they make it. In spring they do it again going back.

Genetic script-writing brings us back to our garden robin, who has not migrated, yet, and is pulling a worm out of earth where I planted the bush. Like starlings, European robins are partial migrants. In winter some leave for Spain, but not all. What makes some stay, some go?

Migration is an adaptive behaviour. It seems to be always on standby and can be triggered by changing conditions: climate change, for instance. Many birds today are altering their migration patterns in response to climate change. Birds are harbingers because they evolve quickly, at least small migrant birds do because their individual lives and species depend on it. Maybe that is what a bird is – always ready.

Does partial migration mean robins are free of the genetic programming which hurls a blackpoll warbler into the maw of a hurricane? No – it is just more complicated. Older robins don't usually migrate. The journey is tough and you have to be up to it, so it is partly age that decides. But mainly the divide is by gender. One sex goes, one stays.

We might expect the boys to go. *The Lotus and the Wind*, John Masters's novel about the Great Game of Anglo-Russian espionage in nineteenth-century Afghanistan, draws a conventional distinction between men – who need freedom, like the wind – and women, who need to be rooted.

Robins play it the other way round. British robins discovered wintering in Spain or Portugal are usually female. Females are smaller and more likely to freeze to death in British winters. Males stay and brave the temperatures. (Or, seen from another perspective, they are dominant over females, so the only way females can survive is to migrate.) For us they become the emblem of Christmas, the gallant little red spark in the blizzard. In reality they are hanging on to their feeding territory till spring.

Chaffinches do the same. The scientific name Linnaeus gave them was *Fringilla coelebs*. In northern Europe, where Linnaeus lived, it is the males you see in winter and *coelebs* is Latin for 'bachelor'.

Many birds go in for partial migration: it may have been a between-stage in every bird's evolution. Some began going; then some did, some didn't. Then they were all doing it, those who didn't died and migrating became an Evolutionarily Stable Strategy: an ESS, a key concept in Game Theory, a way of doing things that sees off any other strategy that comes along.

The robin's great game is partial migration but this is not freedom, nor choice as we know it. A robin's decision is as genetically controlled as a blackpoll warbler's. 'Deciding' is our shorthand for 'programmed by natural selection to behave like this'. Each robin will have its own genetic predisposition to go or stay in a given situation, depending on age, sex, how dominant or adventurous it is, and what's going on outside.

It is with this pseudo-choice of partial migration that the parallel with human beings turns awkward. Is there an innate personality divide that lets some of us uproot easily when faced with a threat, and others not?

Before living in this house and garden we had a flat. Our neighbour in the flat above told me that when she was sixteen in 1930s Berlin, she asked her Jewish parents if they should leave. No, they said. It will be OK. She got the last train out; her parents died.

Go or stay, how do you choose? Going may save you but migrating is a high-risk, high-cost solution. Different family members make different choices. Factors that may tip your fate are age, gender, physical fitness and that complicated, luck-of-the-draw thing, personality – which, for people as well as birds, may partly come down to your genes.

<hr />

However risky the journey, the real struggle starts when you've made it. That's why blackpoll warblers take a short cut through hurricanes and why male robins risk freezing to death. Everything is geared to the battle for resources, not only with each other but with resident species.

This means competition, beak to beak, for the calories. If you film birds at a feeding table and play it back in slow motion you realise how fierce this battle is – as with human immigrants facing residents who resent competition for work, food and homes.

That word 'home' raises a whole spray of questions. What is home, for a bird? We talk about nesting instincts but a nest is not a bird's home. It is where it hatches from the egg and what it makes to lay its own eggs and rear its young. But though some birds return to last year's nest, a nest is only temporary. It is abandoned as soon as possible because for predators – a hungry magpie, for instance – a full nest is an advertisement and a canteen.

Does a bird even have a home? Swifts are Britain's briefest summer migrants. They come in May and are gone by the end of July. When not on a nest they are always in flight. Once a fledgling leaves the nest it will eat, mate and sleep on the wing. A friend of mine who worked in three different spheres once told me, 'I feel most myself when I'm going from one place to another – like a swift.'

Migration means spending your life not only in two different places but also en route. A swallow spends a quarter of its life migrating. Maybe the real home of a swallow or swift is the air; or even the journey, the trajectory.

Some commentators talk of going 'out' from a nesting ground to a winter feeding area and 'back' in spring, but what does this language mean? One bird book on my shelf summons the last ice age to explain the migration of the small northern wheatear. These small birds nest in tundra of the Arctic Circle on several different continents – north Asia, Greenland, Europe, North America. But in winter they all converge, from east, north and west like spokes coming in to the hub of the wheel, on one area of Africa. Why don't those who nest in north Asia fly to south Asia like thousands of other species, and those from North America migrate to South America like the black-poll warbler? Why these long east-west journeys, even over the North Pole?

'Let's admit,' says my bird book, 'this is at heart an African bird which goes north to breed in spring.'

At heart? What does that mean? In the last ice age, says my book, northern wheatears must have stayed in Africa or maybe done a short hop to southern Europe. As the ice left they went further afield (less competition for insects, longer daylight hours to find them) and then edged north. The more adventurous went west and east, but all were still programmed to return to Africa for winter.

But there's something upside-down in this picture. These birds winter in Africa, but does that mean this is where they're 'from'? A Baltimore oriole hatched in Maryland winters in South America: try telling the Baltimore Oriole baseball team their black-and-orange mascot is a South American bird.

Calling the northern wheatear 'African at heart' suggests a peculiarly human and maybe spiritual image: that 'heart' is the end of an outward journey. The tired soul at the end of its life yearns, the Church Fathers said, for its home with God: a mystic home, never yet seen.

People or birds, migrating is all about home. The quest for it, changing it, making it. But maybe where you 'come from' is not as important as who you are at any one moment. One self, one place is not the only model any more than is one self, one language. Just as human beings speak different languages, in different places, so some birds behave differently in different homes. In summer the rufous turtle dove lives in the Himalayas and behaves like a yard bird, foraging for food in villages and farms. In winter it migrates to the Western Ghats in South India where it hides away in deep forest.

Some people live in one home all their lives, but what about first- and second-generation immigrants like my great-grandfather and his children? Is 'home' where your parents came from? Or *their* parents? How far back is back? A friend of mine born in South India taught in Chicago for many years and then moved back to Bangalore. 'My Indian students in Chicago felt American,' she says. 'Their parents came to America when *they* were twenty. My students didn't know Hindi or Gujarati, they didn't feel India was home. They hated it when their parents insisted on going back. I thought it unfair of the parents to ask them to. What was "home" for them felt foreign to the kids.'

The literary theorist and scholar Edward Said was born in Jerusalem. He had an English first name, an Arabic surname, he grew up in Cairo and Lebanon and was Arab but also Christian and Palestinian; and eventually he held an American passport. In his memoir, *Out of Place*, he says he felt at home wherever he was at the time. The Lebanese writer Amin Maalouf grew up in Lebanon but moved to Paris and writes in French. In his memoir *Origins* and his essay *On Identity*, he says he has a different identity in Paris from the one he has when he returns to his native country. Language we use about birds throws up a lot of the questions we ask ourselves about identity, origins and home.

When You're on Your Own

1 Osprey

Goddess of rose-gold pearl behind black cloud,
look after the lonely speck in empty sky
coming in from Senegal to mist over the loch.
One thin cry and she's here too, his mate
from another Africa. May, June, gold-green July –

and she's gone. The male, too. The chick, their brood,
is alone with gravitational pull and evolution
as her guides. France, Spain, North Africa,
Senegal. Fishing demands the quick eye, strong
talon, a spiral on an unscrolled map – and solitude.

2 Hummingbird

Someone has flung rainbow pepper on the air.
The hummingbirds are migrating, each alone:

Blossomcrown, Coppery Thorntail
and Flame-Rumped Sapphire.

They are alone because diet is everything
and you can't queue up for a flower.

They're safe, they're small, most predators
won't see them and a flock would be a target.

They're fearless – they out-manoeuvre everyone
and fly like helicopters

sideways, back, upside down. Pure iridescence:
the dimming light

skimbles like oil film on each metallic green
millimetre of one Ruby-Throat

strimming four hundred and fifty miles
of the Gulf of Mexico

in a twenty-hour dash through the dark
till throat-feathers flash to the rising sun

a sudden spark of bloodroot, cinnabar,
vermilion, puccoon.

That Bird Migration Records the Movement of Earth's Crust

(For Jo)

Overheard at breakfast in the guest house:
'. . . Three millennia of mapping. Furrows
on moonlight and never mind plate tectonics,
how mountains rose in a crash of the lithosphere.
Let continents do their worst – they split,
they clash – but the birds' flight path
is what it always was. Every heartbeat,
every contracting muscle, is a chronicle.'

Bar-headed geese wait for the perfect wind.
All heads turn – each bill
in parallel, rouge compass to a crystal –
towards the cloud-hidden peak. They take off
in a rush. First buffet, and a young one falters . . .
drops . . . The mother checks, wingbeats fail
then pick up – she can't spare – no, cut
to the quick – can't spare a second, tossed

back, up and aslant by djinns
of the mountain. Hurricane gales
force them down to rock and ice.
They sleep, till dawn breaks gold-lattice
through blackshadow cloud. One lifts, a head
out of snow, and now another,

to wind-howl and glare. They stare
at the glacier. Yes, they call. Yes – to try again.

Oxygen speeds like cocaine
through capillaries in deep muscle and here
they come over Everest, gliding down
as if cannonfire ice, the dive-disappear
of a chick she nearly gave her life for
back in Kyrgyzstan and the entire flock's
fall into avalanche were all an absurd
nightmare from which she woke.

Star of the Different Road Back

He's a Zen thinker, clearly: alert
but giving no answers. Opal freckles
on the scatter-breast of an oriental alley cat.
A black velvet cap. Black wing-bars,

sharp orange beak and a back
like rippled rock. Little grey, little grey,
it is spring and all of you
blackpoll warbler brigade

are leaving the dazzle-forests of Venezuela
for fir trees with lichen beards
in Canada. Come September,
you're over the ferocious Caribbean

in the luminous blue upper air
where the Greeks said gods lived
and it's hurricane season. Four days
of battering-ram clouds and slingshot rain

and then the knife-fight for territory?
This is what you flew so far for, and so hard.
A jacaranda pod, blood-
oxide, flowers in the scented dark.

Choice

Digging a bush up, pitching in
to damp earth, getting out
clutch-arms and fingertip veins

as easily broken as silk
I look into the mica eye
of a robin. This is what we say

we all want. The choice –
to go, to stay. But how does a robin
decide? How does anyone?

The Hostile Planet: Sky, Sea, Land

Journeys happen in the air around us all the time, from stars travelling through the night sky to swallows arriving in spring. 'The moon and sun are eternal travellers,' said Bashō. 'Even the years wander on. A lifetime adrift in a boat, or in old age leading a tired horse into the years – every day is a journey and the journey itself is home.'

The sky contains many more aerial migrants than birds. Some which we don't welcome, like locusts, and others who, like fruit bats, disperse seed. These are vital pollinators on which the planet depends, in the silent ecological services by which migration keeps the globe working.

Dragonflies migrate on all continents except Antarctica. North America has nine types of migrating dragonfly: nine arthropod Muses with lovely names like green darner and wandering glider. They fly to Canada in summer cloud-swarms, with tiny writing motions of their wings. The next generation comes back south in the autumn and kestrels migrate with the swarm, snacking on dragonfly along the way.

The longest-known insect journey over sea is from India to the Maldives: millions of globe skimmer and vagrant emperor dragonflies fly fourteen to eighteen thousand kilometres for twenty-four hours against prevailing winds, from South India to east and southern Africa, and back. They breed in temporary rainwater pools, follow the rains from India's monsoons to the short rains of East Africa, summer rains of southern Africa, the long rains of East Africa and back to India for the next monsoon. They eat smaller insects en route while cuckoos, nightjars and falcons follow, with dragonfly on the menu.

Moths, a food source for many creatures, play a key role in the ecosystem and some migrant moths – tiny ones like the diamond-back moth or the twelve-centimetre convolvulus hawkmoth – are important pollinators too. The hummingbird hawkmoth and silver Y come to Britain and Ireland every spring, breed here in summer then go back south to Europe and North Africa.

The Greek word *psyche* means 'soul' but also 'moth'.

<hr />

Most butterflies live only a couple of weeks and never fly far from where they are born. Others live up to nine months and migrate in spring and autumn. Monarchs fly south to Mexico, eighty miles a day at nearly 10,000 feet for 2,000 miles. They arrive around the time of the Mexican Day of the Dead and are greeted as the souls of ancestors. In the spring they go back to northern America. Other migrating butterflies (butterflies and dragonflies get the best names) include the cloudless sulphur, question mark, fiery skipper and mourning cloak. No one knows where their southern migrations end: probably north Mexico, the Gulf Coast and parts of California.

The painted lady is another long-distance migrant to Britain and Ireland from the desert fringes of North Africa, the Middle East and central Asia, but comes variably. Some years you see masses in gardens and meadows, other years hardly any.

Snowdrops are struggling through the frozen earth. In midwinter you feel things will never change. All these hours of darkness! Even at the beginning of February it still feels dark as Christmas. My daughter now has an internship in Bogotá and she says on Skype that the light there is wonderful. But now, by February's end, even Britain is lighter. You know the world has been turning, even though you did not feel it.

Red admiral butterflies come to Britain from North Africa. They used to leave in September, reappear in May and stay for the summer. Now the climate has changed they are seen throughout the year. Before 1990 you'd never have spotted one on a February flower, but today I heard that Britain's Chief Executive of Butterfly Conservation has photographed a red admiral on a snowdrop.

The planet's largest migration happens in the sea every night and morning. It is a vertical migration – billions of jellyfish rise to the surface to feed and sink back down at dawn.

Marine migrants have specialised skills. In 1678, the Italian scientist Stefano Lorenzini noticed rows of dots on the underside of a shark's upper lip; we now know these are gel-filled electro-receptors which detect bands of magnetism in the sea floor. Shark brains are swimming computers, constantly processing data about wave and current patterns, changes in temperature, chemistry, salinity and the Coriolis effect created by the earth as it spins, so the shark can allow for the planet's rotation.

Humpback whales, the globe's farthest-travelling mammals, swim 8,500 kilometres to the equator from breeding grounds at either the North or South Pole, then back again in spring. The total opposite of a barnacle, yet many barnacles attach themselves to ships' hulls or migrating whales and so become long-distance migrants themselves.

But some marine migrations are Go and Stay rather than Go and Come Back. This is where the word 'colonisation' creeps into scientific description.

In 1869 the Suez Canal, built by Ferdinand de Lesseps, cut a channel between two quite different seas. Since then more than 500 marine species, algae, snails, sea slugs and fish, have invaded the Mediterranean from the Red Sea in what is known as Lessepsian migration. It is causing serious ecological problems from Israel to Andalusia. A snorkeller who visits south-west Crete every year told me he now sees in all its little bays the Bluespotted cornetfish (*Fistularia commersonii*) which he first laid eyes on where it evolved, in the coral reefs of the Indo-Pacific.

Salmon, like the rufous turtle dove, develop a different identity in the different places they migrate between. The change is in their bodies as well as behaviour. We are so used to salmon on a plate we forget how extraordinary their life cycle is.

They are spawned in a river. As they migrate down towards the sea they reverse the osmotic functioning of their kidneys and gills to cope with the salt. Then they spend years feeding at sea. Scientists find out where by analysing the chemical signatures trapped in their scales. The salmon change again when they return, years later, to the same river. They give up eating as they swim in from the Atlantic (or Pacific) to the throat of their own river (having survived porpoises, seals, nets, fishermen and weirs) and become 'leapers', straining upriver to reach the ancestral spawning-grounds inland where they all spawn and die. Just as eels born in the Sargasso Sea in the North Atlantic (a sea boundaried only by ocean currents) swim thousands of miles through the Mediterranean, for example, to Lake Ohrid in Macedonia, stay there for years, and then head back to the Caribbean to mate, spawn and die.

Lemmings are very small Arctic rodents, tiny stripy hamsters of black, chestnut and white with long soft hair like the runaway guinea pig in Beatrix Potter's *The Fairy Caravan*. They live in tundra and eat leaves and roots. In winter they burrow through snow and eat grass, which they have sensibly stored in advance. They are shy and solitary. One sixteenth-century geographer thought they fell out of the sky in storms and died when spring grass grew.

Normally they only meet to mate, but their populations fluctuate wildly and when there are too many they disperse en masse. While doing so they sometimes cross rivers, become waterlogged and drown, which gave rise to the myth that they migrate towards mass suicide. So small, so retiring – but responsible for such a potent fantasy, which in 1958 was re-inforced by a master myth-maker.

The 1958 Disney documentary *White Wilderness,* supposedly shot at the Arctic Ocean, won an Academy Award for Best Documentary Feature. Its lemming sequence was filmed at the Bow river in Alberta where no lemmings live, so the film crew brought lemmings from two provinces away in Manitoba and put them on a snow-covered turntable. With tight camera angles, they turned a few pet lemmings cantering on a turntable into a massed mob-gallop over icy tundra.

'Compulsion seizes each tiny rodent,' read the narrator. 'Carried along by unreasoning hysteria, each falls into step for a march that will take them to a strange destiny. They've become victims of an obsession. This is the last chance to turn back yet over they go, casting themselves out bodily into space.'

In fact, the lemmings were thrown into the water; the final shot was of drowning rodents. In 1983 a Canadian documentary exposed what had actually happened. But the myth of mass suicide goes on.

From elephants to emperor penguins, there are hundreds of different kinds of land migration. Crowned lemurs in the deciduous forests of northern Madagascar migrate for miles over eroded mountain limestone karst. European toads struggle several challenging miles over rough ground to find a mate. In upland Sumatra, herds of up to a hundred bearded pigs on their annual migration for food travel at night on paths they have used for centuries, then retreat into thickets to rest in the day and hide from tigers. In North America the reindeer or caribou migrate across lakes and mountains, travelling up to 3,000 miles a year to find food, avoid cold and escape biting insects.

These journeys bring into play the same senses used by birds like sensitivity to earth's magnetic field. Sea turtles approach a nesting beach downwind, drawn by the smell. Migrating bats and porpoises navigate by echolocation, sending out little pulses of sound to map the reflected echoes. Some animals use phonotaxis, the power to pinpoint where sound comes from. The croaks of female toads in a breeding pool drifts through the night air, enticing males to join them. Last year I stood by a shallow stream in the world's only king cobra reserve in the Western Ghats and tracked loud calls echoing through the midnight rainforest down to a half-inch froglet, swelling a pale throat the size of a young pea.

<hr />

All migrations have their dangers. Underneath migrating birds, the worst risks are posed by the desert and the sea. Deserts mean overheating, especially for the all important breast muscles. Some birds stop in the daytime to hide from sun under bushes and refuel. But with drought and overgrazing by starving cattle the deserts are growing; there are fewer shrubs and insects, and less shade.

Many predators evolved to live off migrants. Some follow the travellers, others lie in wait. Whales and zebra migrate with still-suckling babies, who are targetted by lions and killer whales. Europe's largest bat, the greater noctule, which lives in forests from Spain to Turkey, preys off night-migrant birds; sooty falcons time their breeding on Mediterranean cliffs to coincide with the songbirds' autumn migration. The weary birds pass below cliffs where young falcons are honing their hunting skills; adults hang in the air in line and pick off the travellers.

Migrants face, as they have faced for millennia, a hostile planet.

Nocturne

Sundown. I imagine my father,
ten years dead, examining the lilied deep,
a whole marine community
on the move while the planet sleeps.
Zooplankton rise
to graze on surface phytoplankton –
that smudge of green you hardly see
but it's been busy all day
processing the energy of Sun –
followed by a host of arrow worms,
sea butterflies, comb jellies,
larvae. Other tenants of the dark
rise with them, protozoa, copepods
and krill, a ragtag army
preyed on by larger predators still –
the bioluminescence brigade:
lantern-fish glowing cold
catoptromantic rays
three hundred species
of dense-packed cephalopods
and hatchet-fish following
their own fixed upward gaze.

Now he sees torpedoes through the murk.
Sharks, snapping at turtles
oegopsida squid with hooks on the end
of their tentacles and, giant of the deep,

the slow, filter-feeding
eighteen-foot megamouth. Shadows
fighting the task of life in the under-dark
alone. But leading this spout of moon-milk
are the jellyfish. You think of them
don't you as flotsam,
mammary and malign, drifting through waves
which toss them like mermaids on the beach.
But tonight they are the stars
flowering to surface in translucent
violet-rose, a million moons
of tangled crystal, tilted curlicues
of lace. A ghost flotilla,
knots escaping when a manhole cover
is removed. Parachutes, blowing the wrong way,
lenticular galaxies, floaters in the retina,
glass udders trailing a candyfloss whip-
lash of lambent fern.

This is the full mooch skyward,
bubbles of the soul, tendrils of Old Man's Beard
peeling off from the unconscious
in pulp-and-tinsel dribbles,
the book of the sea shredding as it unfolds
and the whole procession white as aluminium –
this suits my dad, he is, after all, a ghost –
or white as the sun when it slips
behind a cloud. A convoy of wraith-buskers
creeping from the Tube

like rebellions of the night. All hail
O jellyfish, you ripple-fringe
of poisoned toga, blip from the cauldron
of nightmare, the unnamed
that is always there under the surface
and what we were always afraid of.
We didn't know for sure but we suspected.
Then, at first light, the delicate descent begins
to a bed we only imagine, the floor
we never see, all heaving crevices
and knuckled weed. The world is not all black
and all white. You are never safe.

The Ampullae of Lorenzini

Who doesn't long
for gel-filled pores
somewhere –
and under your top lip would do –

magneto-receptors, telling you
which geologic line
to follow
clean below Orion

over the East Nazareth Mountains
into some Gangetic Sea,
Cathay, Shangri-La or Eldorado
and along the seabed, home?

Barnacle's Love Song
to Humpback Whale

It's chaos out there, but my single eye
tells dark from light and nothing else
needs to be seen. There are no boundaries
or pattern, it's an anarchy I'm floating in
and I rely on cirri. My feathery appendages
reach into the water-column, froth it
like cappuccino, draw plankton into my shell.

I have no heart. But a series of muscles, salt
velvet origami, pump blood through my sinus
and oxygen comes through membrane
lining my carapace. I am always at home
upside down. Armoured in concentric rings
of lustrous plates, my gates of heaven,
I slide a shutter to keep out the world beyond.

What does connection matter? My ovaries
extend like angels' wings from my mantle
to jellied base; my testes run nape to thorax.
I have the longest penis, relative to body size,
in the world. When I was larva
being adrift was a blizzard of risk. Free,
before tying the knot, to probe potential surfaces.

You've only one shot: I hitched my wagon
to everything I'm not. Life on the move.

At the North Pole in summer, we gorge
on nutrients, he and I.
Through the radiator grill of his baleen
he takes in shoals of krill like whiskery paper clips.
We share the translucent zooplankton

welling like gladioli in three-mile plumes
off the arctic floor. While he puts on
ten tons of blubber, I decorate
his stratum corneum and epidermal layer.
When the temperature drops
we race for the equator. He flings
himself loose of the sea and we're in free fall.

Who hasn't seen us burst like a raga to the Sun –
a prayer in dancing turquoise –
and lob our tail-fluke down (he's laughing, look)
to smack the shawling foam? That's me up there
riding his leap, hub to his wheel of black air.
And we make music. Those world-class,
bourrées, gigues and habañeras are composed for me.

I ripple to his tunes like castanets
but my own songs are only for him:
my fifty-foot wanderer, my ocean troubadour,
my Ararat. I am his *petit point*
embroidery. From his ventral groove
and under-jaw, I console
his mammal heart, his loneliness.

In Praise of Eight Million Fruit Bats

Here's to eight million straw-coloured fruit bats
living cheek-by-mouse-jowl in colonies
at the edge of forest, on the fringe
of cities all through Africa; who converge
for November and December on the dark border

with Congo, one skid-scented corner
of Kasanka National Park, to gorge themselves on fruit
and then fly off, *syrop*-filled dancing particles
dizzy as customers at the bar of the Electric Ballroom:
heroes, jittering a boogaloo, strobing the skies like a
                                                    twister

to disperse manure, scat, soft serve, butt drool,
Gatling gun, jailbreak Havana omelette
and butt burrito, their little dingleberry brownies –
that's sixty per cent, to you and me, of seed
that pollinates all the rainforest in Africa.

The Miracle of the Fish-Counter
in Budgens

All face the same way, tear-proof painted enamel
laid out on crumbled ice like a racing shoal –
of, let's say, salmon. I see them migrating

from the wild Atlantic or Pacific
they've known for five years, maybe six,
back to the river where they hatched

to leap together in parallel, just like this,
hurling their silver-paper forms against the exact
current which swept them down when they were smolts

before their mystery began, that metamorphosis
from fresh to salt when their kidneys changed,
gills reversed the direction of their frantic pulse

and the adult fish shot into open sea. And now,
changing again, they eat no more, burning the energy
sea-stored in years of freedom, for the release

of spawning: to reproduce in turn the perfect
workmanship we pass, dreamwalking
through the supermarket's mazy hieroglyph,

all this crinkled glitter, each mirror-glazed button-eye
stamped on the ice like a mourning brooch
collecting the glare of the strip light.

Or eels, born in the shoreless sea, who journey
a thousand miles then thousands more
through the bruised Mediterranean

to Ohrid and Crni Drim, to live in lake-mud glue
like a man who has forgotten how to love,
then suddenly return

thousands of sea miles again
to the Caribbean. As if go home and breed,
go home and die were the norm.

Ethogram for a Painted Lady

I'm six and we are *keeping still.*
We're looking at shadow on grey stone
in the sunken garden
and an orange-black fan – two fans, really,
with dribbles of milk on each tip
and a bravura range of little eyespots –

looking back at us. I have never heard
of Morocco, or anything outside this strip
of Eden with its secret sundial
I thought only I knew,
but I will remember standing here
with my grandmother, watching

flying blossom of the meadow
sun itself. Maybe I'm there still,
I never left;
I've never heard of Morocco
where these guys stream in from
steering by polarised light into Europe

over the Straits of Gibraltar,
funnelling in on the shortest sea crossing
like eagles gliding from thermal to thermal
on the same route;
a million-thick cloud of half-inch souls
swarming to the fields of asphodel.

Blade Runners of Madagascar

Did I dream them up? Those lemurs on late-night TV
pelting for days, striped tails like silver-and-black
bananas held high; the babies leaping too
or missing their step and falling one side or the other,
furry limbs bouncing through four
thousand metres of drop, through turrets

of tropical forest, lianas wrestling them down
in true no-holds-barred kung fu to the jaws
of pythons below. It's a hurtle for miles
over limestone pinnacles, raw knife-edges
scraping the sky, in a race for a safe place –
the good place – to breed, feed and rest.

Road Closed to Save Mating Toads

Listen, children. If you're out late afternoon,
just before the first warm wet evening of spring,
you'll hear a rustle in leaves at the side of the road.
That'll be the male toads, crawling from
your gardens, from hedgerows and ditches,
back to the pond where they were tadpoles.
When they reach the water they begin to sing
and to this male-voice chorus, trilling away
like nobody's business, come the amber-eyed females

drawn from the silent woods by a fusion
of phonotaxis, trigonometry and hormones.
It's a life-and-death affair, this half-mile crawl
in straight lines, toes spread for good contact
with earth, struggling through rough grass, power
lines, slip roads and a motorway. When a female arrives
the males grab with warty tubercles
on their fingers, to get a tight amplexus. And the whole
joyous event tends to coincide with the rush hour.

Chemical

There were stories of mountain goats in Montana
climbing sheer cliffs for a lick of salt

and brocket deer wading in Amazon quicksand
pumping their front legs to stop sinking

and suck the rich mineral upwellings.
We flow to what we need, they said.

Elephants in Kenya march their young
through tunnels under Mount Elgon.

It's no stroll in the park, they said. Pitch dark
and the boulders are slippy and loose.

The elephants feel the slime-walls with their trunks,
play blind man's buff with the stalactites

and can't see a thing, but remember the treadings
from last year, from all years, steering

with giant foot-glands right to the core,
the great dead-end heart of salt rock

then going at it, gouging it out
with their tusks. Listen to them crunch,

crunch, crunch for their life.
The babies are bored,

they play with stones they cannot see
but remember this gash in their lives,

this every-year-a-bit-longer inward journey
under the mountain, into the dark.

There is Always a River

Today *seven* goldfinches on the feeders, the most I've ever seen: a charm of goldfinches. They form little flocks in winter but now, in March, they must have several nests close by. But we have to say goodbye to them. My daughter will be home in a couple of months, but then she'll go back to Colombia to work for a year or two and without her our beloved house and garden are too big. We've got to look for something smaller.

I should be house-hunting. Instead, I'm looking back to Africa where Britain's nightingales and swallows still are, where *Homo sapiens* and human migration began, and where I watched the climax of the three-month trek over the Masai Mara endured by wildebeest, zebra and Thomson's gazelles.

From a parked jeep on a riverbank in Kenya I saw a scene which summed up for me the unstoppable pull of migration. It was early morning, the air still cool. The sun had only just got up. Below was the Mara River, the end of the animals' journey. Nothing stirred – then three absurdly delicate Thomson's gazelles, a buck and two does, arrived. They stopped on a flat stretch of shore and stared at the shining water. The river drew them. They could hardly bear to glance away to check for lions.

I had come to Kenya to see one of the wonders of the world – a million and a half wildebeest, 300,000 Burchell's zebra (Plains zebra) and 50,000 of these gazelles, finishing their annual trek.

Words migrate too: 'trek' is Afrikaans, from Dutch *trekken*, 'to journey, to pull'. It means 'to travel or migrate by ox-wagon'. The *Groot Trek* began in 1835, when 10,000 Boers fed up with English rule left the Cape Colony and went north. These gazelles had trekked north too from Tanzania and the river was their last obstacle.

Everything was quiet. The fairy-like gazelles – our guide called them Tommies – tiptoed to the water's edge, flirted away and then came back, tails flicking side to side. There is a scent gland under their tail: wagging it sheds scent to spread alarm.

I watched the flicking tails and thought about rivers, the last barrier in so many stories of escape. I thought about magic objects you throw down behind, the mirror or handkerchief which turns into a river to block your pursuers. About the Red Sea parting to let through the Israelites following Moses away from Egypt and into the wilderness; and, four books of the Old Testament later, the Jordan River stopping its flow as the Israelites follow Joshua out of the wilderness. The priests carry the Ark of the Covenant into the water and the people follow through it safe and dry, over to the Promised Land.

Rivers are natural borders. Mexican immigrants to the United States are called wetbacks because they swim the Rio Grande to get there. Rivers are often sacred, too. Hermann Hesse's novel *Siddhartha* tells the story of the Buddha leaving home to learn the world. He crosses a river in a forest and years later he returns to become the ferryman on the same river, which represents life flowing on to its goal. In Hinduism, pilgrimage sites are crossing-places. The sacred place to which the pilgrims are journeying is the *tirtha*, which originally meant 'crossing-place' or 'ford' and now (whether the place you head for has a ford or not) means simply 'pilgrimage'; for pilgrimage itself is a crossing.

For the Ancient Greeks, the River Styx was the crossing from life to death and that morning in Kenya we could see death waiting for the gazelles in a silver ripple.

They had come from the Serengeti, following hundreds of thousands of zebra and even more wildebeest in the greatest migration of mammals on the planet.

In March or April the Serengeti grass dries up and herds of these three species begin drifting north, following the rain, occasionally cantering, often walking with bowed heads, following a pheremone trail laid by scent glands in the hooves of those ahead.

Large groups stay together like flocking birds. As with jellyfish rising to the surface of the sea, scavengers and predators follow: lions, cheetah, hyena, jackal, wild dogs, insects, parasites and birds who perch on wildebeest backs to get out the ticks.

The wildebeest thrive because of their enormous numbers. They are stupid and helpless as individuals but successful as a herd because they do everything at the same time. Females drop their calves in the Serengeti all at once. Two-thirds of them survive simply because the waiting predators are glutted.

Darwin's principle again – nature is indifferent to the individual and frighteningly wasteful, but the species survives.

For lions and other predators, the long columns are a walking canteen. When they attack there is a stampede, calves get separated, kicked, disabled and then lost. I saw one lying on its side in burning sun, feebly twitching the hooves it was never going to stand on again. Even without predators, exhausted young zebras fade with hunger, heat and thirst. Clear pools turn to mud as they walk through, the sun bakes the mud into a shell and traps weak calves.

As they go, the wildebeest keep in touch with a sound like burping. *Erb. Erb* . . . it is a froggy moo, a million-strong conversation like that of migrating geese. In June and July they reach the Masai Mara, stop on the banks of the Mara and stare at fresh grass on the far side.

The crossing is not just one event. There is not one herd but dozens in different places all along the Mara. Groups of all three species kept arriving, congregating at different spots along the bank.

The day before, we had watched thousands of wildebeest mill round on the bank, kicking up dust clouds. They had burped their way from the Serengeti and now, weary after months of travel, faced the river. If they were human you'd have said they were plucking up courage. It wasn't deep. It would take three minutes to splash through to the grass they smelt. But they knew, whatever knowing meant inside those bearded heads, that there was danger.

There were hippos upriver, but hippos keep themselves to themselves. The Masai say hippos spend the day telling each other jokes on the riverbed and rise up at night to laugh at them. There were six different types of vulture, too, walking about on the bank among the herds, as tall as a calf's withers. The wildebeest ignored them but the reason they were here (as well as hundreds of tourists, waiting in jeeps along both banks like spectators at a Formula One meeting) lay hidden in the water, where the largest crocodiles in Africa awaited their summer banquet.

The stage was set. It was up to the wildebeest. Crowds of them built up on the bank, jostling from behind like a stadium audience. Sometimes a crossing begins when one animal is pushed off the bank by pressure of numbers. One male tip-toed down to the edge, snorted at the surface, swung round and cantered up the bank again. They jostled as he joined them, skipped and reformed their crowd, facing the river.

Another herd came up behind and suddenly another male leaped into the water, landed with a belly flop and thrashed towards the far bank. The water came just above his tummy. Clouds of fawn dust rose as hundreds plunged in after him. Calves went in over their shoulders, swimming. It was Follow My Leader, a distillation of programmed compulsion. Dust on the bank turned to mud, calves were trampled as the herd came pouring down.

Then the crocodiles moved in. As they pulled wildebeest under the water the vultures came to life. Perching on animals which had been alive beside them five minutes before – now carcasses sticking on boulders – they spread their huge wings to balance.

Cameras whirred.

The centre of the river became clogged with dead wildebeest. A pale-blue mountain wagtail flicked down to get food for her young. A weaver bird picked off ticks crawling away from the dying.

There were no zebra that day. Zebras are stronger and more intelligent: wildebeest often follow their lead. Zebras cross as they migrate, in family groups. A blow from a zebra hoof could disable a jaw, so experienced crocodiles wait for the wildebeest and take just the odd timid mare or foal which hangs back and gets isolated.

Most zebra make it. So do most wildebeest, because there are so many. But their crossing is pure carnage.

The gazelles come last. They, too, cross in small groups, but they are smaller, they have to swim. Only zebras are brainy enough to calculate entrance and exit from the river and these gazelles had picked a place where they could not possibly scramble out: the far bank was a sheer black cliff.

<hr />

The male gazelle took his first step into the shallows, bounced in on impossibly cotton-thin legs, stopped and looked back and then gazed at the far side, a wall he could never conceivably climb. He was knee-deep. You could almost see a magnet on the other bank pulling.

This is it, I thought. The pull of the world. Migration in action. From higher up we could see an enormous crocodile drifting slowly towards him. Water refraction must have made it invisible to the gazelle. Gazelle brains and eyes did not evolve to wonder about water and what lies beneath. They evolved for the plains, to see a long way and keep alert to whatever lion might be hiding behind the next anthill.

He wheeled round, the does flitted and flinched – and all three ended up staring at the river again. Suddenly he started swimming. He was a clockwork gazelle doing a splashy butterfly. He was little and had chosen the deepest place to cross. The females watched, their faces filled with him, tiny hooves standing in the choppy waves he made, their reflections trembling beside the shore they were driven to leave. There was a slash of brown lightning, a split-second open jaw and their boy was gone.

Crocodiles pull prey under the water to drown it. There was barely a struggle. The two does looked at water-gleam resettling on the surface. They'd watched him go and now he wasn't there.

⸻

What compels them is the grass. They migrate for food and water in a continual cycle through the year. The three species act on the land like a giant lawnmower whose dung puts energy back in the soil, keeping the all-important grass stimulated with nutrients.

Most grass-eaters live in herds, balancing competition for resources against the advantages of being many: more eyes on the look-out for danger, more voices to give the alarm.

Those that make it over the Mara instantly begin to feed, like birds after a 6,000-mile migration. Grass is armoured against grazing teeth by hair-flakes of silicon, which wear down ivory teeth, but the tough teeth of zebra strip the top rough stems, the wildebeest go for the lower stalks and the latecomers, the little Tommies, nibble the lowest tenderest shoots which the others have laid bare.

Come October, however, the rains will trigger their return. They will all surge back through this hard-won river. Crocodiles cull hundreds – but hundreds of thousands get through and trek south to the grass plains of the Serengeti.

Why go back? Why another Mara crossing, another dangerous journey, when grass still surrounds them like bright fur?

They go because mammals need minerals. We look for gold, bauxite, iron and oil in the earth, but wildebeest, zebra and gazelles look for the phosphorus they find only in the Serengeti, in the soil of Ngorongoro. The Serengeti grass was just withered stalks when they left it behind nine months ago, but now they need it again, to absorb the phosphorus and bear their young in a cycle that never stops. Twice a year they are driven to cross, to face the crocodiles. All for a mineral, all for a phosphate.

Song of the Herbivores

Even grass defends itself. Hair-flakes of silicon
armour the blades, making the aerial culm
and its inflorescence a cutting edge
of gritty emerald, wearing all ivory down.

We open our dental roots so teeth can go on
growing. Alone on an open plain, in the whisper
of long grass, you're easy meat for wild dog,
hyena, lion, so let there always be somebody's head

raised up, always a rolling eye, an ear
cocked. Stamp, snort; shed alarm
through your scent-gland. Paw earth,
toss your head, drop dung and follow the herd

to the sweet brachiating seed-pod,
dry peeling kernel, stem-moult and mineral
rise in fresh sap, in the battle
to not get eaten, the battle to eat.

Zebra Go First

They've spent the wet season on Tanzania's soil
where phosphorus bleeds oil through grass-veins
in Serengeti. Now the rains fail, waterholes
shrink and dry, they start moving away.
Long columns trek to the river
and beyond. He is Moses, a stallion,

black pigment blazon
over homozygous white. For six miles behind
they hang heads in a dustcloud and follow.
He is energy, razor heels in sorrel dust,
yellow teeth bared on this stream of striped ponies
in their thirst, their great thirst, for the north.

Dream of the Zebra Foal

Head lower, then lower under a lenticular
dark cloud, he drags harlequin fetlocks
through the pimpling dust. Slower, then slower
through night ringed with eyes,
this soot and fester theatre of leopard
and caracal, watching him weaken. All he knows

is that he doesn't know, and is afraid
of moon-shadow where the great rocks part;
where heat detectors crowd
the auditorium of the midnight plains.
Predator cilia radar in on flesh
that does not know it glows, it draws.

Let's give him one dream-memory,
one zebra wish fulfilled
in a green wall of sugarcane.
And look, he's made it through
to the rose-bleach and blaze of dawn.
One more day nearer the water.

Wildebeest Calf

A red sun falls under tick-filled blond grass
through curves in dun stalks and the ear-outline
of a low-slung lion. Chestnut eyes are making a choice.
Bee-eaters leave the *croton* bush – a squawk
of crown plovers – then a scuffle, thud, gurgle.
A bellow; a cry cutting caramel skies.

Night. And the soft breath beside him, the horns
that kept away danger, have gone. *Bleat.*
Losing the herd, he lingers to morning.
No milk. *Bleat.* Calling for comfort.
Here comes a stallion's zebra-kick
stopping the cry that draws predators.

His front leg hangs from his knee.
Afternoon – and he's alone, first time
in his life, flat on earth,
ribs grazing the sky. Glistering flies.
He scrabbles; he waits in a daze
for vultures, jackals and dusk.

Vulture Optics

Raising chicks in the dry season,
spreading gloss wings to mantle
hot hungry fledglings, he guides
red gut-threads into ever-wide maws.

Through their clamour for more, he checks
from the cliff on herds he has followed
for weeks, alert for signs of weakening.
His wide-angle eye keeps shifting, as if he saw

all body-mass through the background swirl
of Thomas Bewick, focussing
on just this knee-buckle, flop-flurry
of a foal, and the mare's hanging head:

her black whiskers puzzling, her breath
stirring fur on a thin tummy heaving
where stripes fade to cream.
She's been all his shelter. Her jaw

shadows his face, now cheek to cheek
with the earth. The herds file past, seven miles
of smoke-yellow glare. She must follow or die.
The stallion snakes his thick neck;

teeth draw blood on her buttock
locking her back to the herd.
As she leaves, ants cluster
on moisture – nose mucus, eye membrane

and a fluttering lid – while vulture-wings
rattle. Now the curved beak
plunges, tasselling to shreds
the opened muscle. A foal, a living feast.

The Mara, Rising

Water slaps lolling tongues, cools the dry throats.
Stop, look around, look up and behind

then gulp, gulp, suck. Jigsaw muzzles
join their own reflection

in bombazine blistered with rain.
Above, the marbling rapids. Sand martins

and swallows in hollows of the bank.
Below, the largest crocodiles in Africa.

How Does a Zebra Decide?

Over the river are rains and the grass.
At his back the hot herds jostle.
They've come five hundred miles
for this rattle-flow over grey stone.
Striped faces stare at the rock.
He paws the beach-sludge, splashes; stops
at one flash-memory of slaughter.
He swings his head down, then up
with a knee-flex and crazing of bubbles.
The weak, the hesitant won't make it.
He plunges, a reel in the eddies,
a stagger in rust-colour mud –
and he's steady in a breast-high current.
Whirlpools of white mark the spot
where each fetlock enters the water.

Pregnant Gazelle

You're in your worst dream.
An hour to giving birth
and you've got to get over a river
piled with split bodies. She opts

for the rapids' sharp rocks
and struggles alone through the hiss-slap
of foam. She wasn't made for swimming.
She's used to the herd, not this roar

of cirrus spray, an under-whirl tug
to the waterfall, the sluice, the crocodiles.
But she makes it, she joins the hundreds
that got through. By the time she heaves

out of the river and drops her fawn,
zebra molars are stripping the serrate
leaf margins of new grass
and rough cauline outer layers

and ten thousand wildebeest
grazing lower axils, where each petiole
joins the stem, have exposed
the glabrous shoots, bracts, umbels,

the branching lobes, paired glumes
and tender root-scales
of spikelets she can eat. Her son
wags his black tail, a ticking pendulum

that'll only stop when life ends,
and starts to nurse. The world
stands over them. The trek
begins and ends. Begins again.

History's Push and Pull

'Look at that!' Two bright green parakeets zoom through the April fizz of white blossom, shrieking. The plumber stops servicing the boiler and we both stand marvelling at this flash of tropical palette.

Rose-ringed parakeets evolved in the tropics. They live from West Africa to India; I've seen them in the Western Ghats and Mumbai. But they began escaping from captivity in Britain and establishing flocks here in the 1970s and now feature on CDs of British garden birdsong. They have survived the snow and here they are in our own (though not ours for much longer) backyard. They dangle opposite each other like emerald shoulders of a translucent heart. The male has a beautiful pink necklet. The tits and goldfinches have vanished: there's only room for so many birds. Darwin, thinking of the ruthlessness of competition, compared nature to a yielding surface with 10,000 sharp wedges packed close together and driven inwards, sometimes one wedge, sometimes another, by incessant blows.

Ornithologists worry about the effect these parrots are having on our birds, both resident and migrant. Who do they compete with for food and nest holes: woodpeckers, starlings, nuthatches? If these stick around, our goldfinches won't get so much food and will raise fewer babies this year.

Human history, like that of the plants and animals, is a story of migration. But compared to the animals' slow subtle adaptations to the spin of the globe, our history is perhaps – as Vermeer suggests when he represents History as a maenad in his picture *The Art of Painting* – less balanced.

Some human beings live by Go-and-Come-Back migration. Herders move flocks to higher pasture for summer and to the valley in winter, up and down the mountain like Himalayan pheasants. Many Greeks who left for Australia generations ago return to the family island for three or four summer months. More generally, people go where the work is. Our morning and evening commuting in and out of cities across the globe mirrors the daily ascent and descent of jellyfish. Like birds following migrating wildebeest for insects, migrant workers travel wherever there are crops to be picked or roads to be built. Gabriel García Márquez's story 'Leaf Storm' describes the arrival at a small town in Caribbean Colombia, in 1909, of a foreign banana company followed by 'the chaff of a civil war' – men hoping for work carrying 'their single piece of baggage, a wooden trunk or bundle of clothing'. Specialised workers, stonemasons, glass-blowers, entertainers and musicians like my great-grandfather Christian, have always moved from town to town.

What we mainly do as a species, however, is Go and Stay. We spread out of Africa just as animals spread, in search of territory. The ancient sign for wagon, carved into crags across mountains and plains, tells archaeologists the ways we went. Young tigers disperse from parents to find territories of their own and avoid inbreeding: so do we. Plants spread and so do we. 'Diaspora' is a 'seeding across', and we have seeded every continent.

⠿⠿⠿⠿⠿⠿⠿⠿

But with human beings, Go and Stay needs some redefining. Animal and plant migration is various. It may be done by individuals or groups, may take place once in a lifetime, seasonally or every day, but at its heart is a search for something that you can't get at home. Migration is going where the thing is which you need but don't have. There is a push and a pull. You are drawn to the other side of the river, to the grass, but are also escaping what's on this side: drought.

All this is true also of *Homo sapiens*, but with extra complexities. Human migration is about not only need but want. Our wants are more unpredictable than those of animals and plants, and there are two ways of taking that word. If you're *in* want, you don't have enough – your family will die if you don't migrate. If you've always lived off fish and there are no more fish – as today on the coasts of Somalia and Senegal – you send your young men to Europe to get money to feed the family.

But human beings want more than they physically need and their search for what is lacking at home is more varied and ambiguous than that of the animals. We want spiritual and educational sustenance, for instance. Folk 'long', according to Chaucer, to go on pilgrimage; ancient pilgrimage routes run all over Europe, the subcontinent and the Middle East. We also take seasonal group journeys as tourists for pleasure; and many of us go abroad to school.

Last night I asked an Australian friend who lives in England if she thought she was a migrant. No, she said. Why not? 'Because I didn't *have* to come.'

'You came to Europe,' said her English husband, 'because you wanted to go to university in Paris. That was something you couldn't do at home. You did have to come – there was something you needed. Besides me,' he added.

Unlike most other life forms, we want more territory and possessions than we need. A tiger does not want more territory than it needs but we, or some of us, do. This means that human migration is inextricably mixed with trade, invasion, conquest and empire. Some migrations are a spreading to get more; others are escape from foreign incursions.

Of all the pull-and-push factors behind migration, war is one of the greatest. The Second World War created 40 million refugees. While Napoleon invaded Spain, during the Peninsular War of 1808–14, Goya etched his sequence *The Disasters of War*. On two of the etchings (of refugees fleeing famine in Madrid) he wrote, 'I saw it', and 'And this too.' His painting *The Colossus* dates from the same time. The terrified refugees fleeing from a naked giant, who appears to be blindly roaming the Spanish countryside, sum up the push factor behind migration. If your house, city, country or temple is destroyed and something terrible has entered your landscape, all you can do is run.

⸻

Hope is the great pull – but there is usually a push factor behind it. Hopes are born, says John Berger, the great writer on migration, on the site of loss. Most stories we tell about past migrations, or more largely where human beings came from and how they spread, invoke a violent loss.

According to the Bible, human wandering began with the loss of Eden. Subsequently, Noah's sons spread out and populated different quarters of the globe, but only after the rest of humanity was wiped out. In Michaelangelo's painting of the Flood in the Sistine Chapel, the Ark floats safely away while refugees desperate to escape the rising waters climb trees on a mountaintop and cling to a capsizing hull.

In Greek myth, Europe began with a raped Lebanese princess. In the Bronze Age you'd have called her Phoenician: Europa descended from the Asian people who first navigated the Mediterranean and gave Greece its alphabet. Her father ruled a coastal city south of where Beirut now stands. Its name meant 'Rock' – *Sur* in Phoenician and *Tzor* in its sister language Hebrew. The Greeks called it Tyre. Myth said that Zeus, the king of the gods, disguised himself as a bull, kidnapped Europa and swam with her to Crete where he raped her and so founded the house of Minos. European culture, therefore, begins with a kidnap, a rape (which literally means a 'snatching') and a forced migration – like the forced migration of enslaved Africans which created African American culture.

The Trojan War was caused by a kidnap in the opposite direction when Helen, wife of a Greek prince, was carried east by a Trojan to Troy. The Greeks' war to get her back created the West's first great image of a fallen city. Troy, the beautiful walled city, is burned, its women are enslaved and Prince Aeneas sails to Italy, a refugee. He is blown off-course to North Africa but crosses to Sicily and then on to Italy, where he founds a new city and new civilisation – Rome.

Homer's *Odyssey*, icon of twentieth-century imagination, is a long homecoming and a painful reassertion of identity: the war veteran returns. But Virgil's *Aeneid* is a story for the twenty-first century: the displaced man who has seen his city burn and has lost one identity forever must make a new home and a new identity in an unknown land. Civilisation is the story of building but also of losing. Behind the arrival in a new land often stands catastrophe and destruction. London was a Roman *colonia*, a colony or 'settled land': the word comes from *colere*, 'to inhabit, to cultivate'. But the Romans used it to translate Greek *apoikia*, which also means a colony, but meant literally, 'being away from home'. For Aeneas, Rome itself was 'being away' from his burnt home.

⸻

The historical Greeks who colonised Asia Minor in the seventh century BC migrated for trade. Trade moved over deserts, mountains and seas – the Sahara, the Himalayas, the Mediterranean, the Indian Ocean – and migration follows. Religion follows, too. It was traders who brought Hinduism to Indonesia in the fifth century AD, Buddhism soon after and Islam from 1200 onward.

Christianity, however, was set up to spread from the start. 'Apostle' comes from Greek *apostellein*, 'to send out', and the Apostles spread Christianity through the Roman Empire. In 1095 this became a violent spreading: the First Crusade began centuries of war (mainly against Muslims, but also against Jews and Orthodox Christians) for Catholic control of the Holy Land.

People migrate to spread their own religion ('missionary' comes from the Latin *mittere*, 'to send') but also to escape other people's. In 1492 the Inquisition expelled the Jews from Spain (or forced them, and Spanish Muslims, to turn Catholic). In 1620 the Pilgrims boarding the *Mayflower* were escaping religious persecution: they wanted a place to worship as they pleased.

Trade and religion *can* move without war, but often arrive because of it. Before the Second World War, Coca-Cola was bottled in forty-four countries. After US troops landed in North Africa in 1943, General Eisenhower requested ten bottling plants there. At the end of the war the troops went home but Coca Cola stayed. Sixty-four new plants were shipped abroad during the war; by the 1960s the number of countries with bottling operations had doubled.

Did oak trees spread to England after the ice age, or colonise it? Shift the language and you shift the perspective. Even with algae and fish, that word 'colonise' entails pushing out what's been there before, like marine species from the Red Sea triumphing over Mediterranean fish. A successful human colony or settlement means turfing someone else out; or else killing them, enslaving them or taking them over. For residents, the advent of a new species or tribe means invasion; as the City of Sydney recently acknowledged when in its formal account of its history it changed the words 'European arrival' to 'European invasion'. 'In respect to the Aboriginal community,' said the Lord Mayor, 'it's very important.'

In histories of many other civilisations you find the words 'The X Invasions'. Han Tribes into ancient China, Dorians into ancient Greece, Mongols, Normans, Vikings, conquistadors, Pilgrim Fathers – they rode, sailed or walked into other lands and created a new culture on top of – and often at the expense of – something else. Unless there's been an ice age or a Great Flood, there's no clean slate.

Sixteenth- and seventeenth-century European migrations into new lands, and the trade routes which European powers developed in order to reach them, shaped the modern world. By the 1580s Spain controlled Mexico's two most valuable exports, silver and cochineal. Wealth was pouring into Spain from the West Indies and South America while Britain, Holland and Portugal were competing to send adventurers into other lands for gold, spices and timber, and to control the sea routes that led to them. Meanwhile, in the East, empires and trade networks rose and fell between and through India, China, Japan and South East Asia, creating new migrations.

Walter Raleigh dreamed of colonising America. He tried to

go in the early 1580s, but had to turn back. The expeditions he went on later (drawn by rumours of a City of Gold) were to South America. But between 1584 and 1590 he was the prime mover in the first colonial expeditions to North America. These are now known as the Roanoke Voyages, since their base was Roanoke Island within the Carolina Outer Banks.

In 1585 the expedition artist was John White, commissioned to 'draw to life' the inhabitants of the New World and their environment. He painted in watercolour (unusually – most painters preferred oil-based paint) and seventy-five of his water-colours survive, showing villages, harbours, crops, fish, wild birds and people: the sixteenth-century, south-eastern Algonquins who inhabited what is now North Carolina and South Virginia. One thing I love about White's portraits – women and children, husbands and wives – is their warm smiles. They seem easy and natural with the artist and each other.

But relations with the villagers, at first so friendly, deterio-rated. Over the next five years, things were to go very wrong.

The first expedition returned with tobacco (which Raleigh popularised) and the potato, which Raleigh introduced to Ireland. Two years later Raleigh encouraged White to go back as Governor, leading a proper colony of settlers including White's daughter Eleanor and her husband Ananias Dare, whom she had just married at St Bride's Church in Fleet Street.

But their Portuguese pilot refused to take them on to Chesapeake Bay as arranged, and abandoned the settlers on Roanoke Island. Eleanor gave birth to a daughter, Virginia, but White himself had to return to England for supplies and couldn't get back to the island for three years: all boats were commissioned to fight the Spanish Armada. He returned on 18 August 1590, his granddaughter's third birthday. The settlers had gone, but the letters CRO were carved on a tree, possibly as a sign that they were safe, and had moved on to Croatoan Island.

This was the mystery of the 'lost colony', the earliest attempt at a permanent English settlement in America. No one knows if they survived. White retired sorrowfully to Raleigh's estates in Ireland where the English were meanwhile displacing other indigenous inhabitants.

⸻

In 1585 Queen Elizabeth knighted Raleigh for his help in 'putting down' a rebellion in Ireland. She also gave him estates in Munster. Further north in Ireland, the English were slower to take control. Before the 1590s Ulster was thickly forested with few towns or roads. Many people there lived by seasonal migration with their cattle. From 1594 several chieftains fought the English incursions, but in 1603 they had to surrender. In 1607 came the Flight of the Earls, when the chieftains left for the continent. The English began planning settlements. 'Settling' sounds calm but this was a violent, invasive colonisation, displacing the inhabitants, dispossessing them, driving them into marginal mountain land and replacing them with English-speaking Protestants. But many stayed to work for these new owners on land they had once owned: hence the patchwork of Protestant-Catholic settlements, and the enduring antagonism in Ulster.

This was just about the time that the word 'migrate' is first recorded in English, used of people. The settlers were told that the natives would be eradicated, but the woodkerne, men who had lost their lands and fought the English, hid in forests and carried on fighting until they were killed, deported, or accepted English-speaking rule.

At the Battle of the Boyne in 1690, William of Orange ensured Protestant English rule over the whole of Ireland. Thousands of Irish who had fought for Catholic King James left to serve him in France and became known, as we have seen, as 'The Wild Geese': the title of the Irish Brigade in foreign armies throughout Europe and South America, and today the name of the Irish cultural society in America; wild geese who never returned.

On the continent, Europe entered a new wave of religious conflict in 1567, when the Netherlands finally rose against Spanish rule. This was three years before Pieter Bruegel died. The run-up to the Eighty Years War, and Spanish persecution of Protestants, formed the background to his last decade of painting.

Bruegel's peasant scenes, his strange brand of social criticism and allegory which earned him the nickname 'Pier den Drol', Pieter the Droll, are landscape-free. Their point is people and their behaviour. But Bruegel had seen the Alps when he went to Italy as a young man, and when he painted religious and mythical stories he often set them in Alpine landscape which somehow claims more of our attention than the human drama it contains. In *Landscape with the Fall of Icarus* (1562) the lush Italianate scenery is the foreground while in the middle, very small, is the failed refugee. The son of a man trying to bring his child safely away from Crete, is drowning in the sea.

Bruegel also displaced on to older stories the cruelty he saw around him. In 1568, after war had begun, he painted *Massacre of the Innocents*, setting the story – women weeping over slaughtered babies, families begging in vain for their lives, soldiers breaking into homes – in his home town of Antwerp. Five years before, he had invoked Alpine scenery to paint what was happening while that massacre took place: Joseph leading Mary and child secretly away on a donkey. European artists had painted the *Flight into Egypt* since the eighth century: the holy asylum-seekers save their baby from persecution in an archetypal escape from a Colossus. The scene is the New Testament echoing the Old: one family seeking refuge in the country from which Moses led his whole persecuted people.

Many painters of this scene showed pagan idols slipping from their shrines as the child went by, and so did Bruegel. He set the scene high in summer mountains. Mary's eyes are turned down, Joseph has his back to us and the baby is hidden but the landscape tells us as much, or more, than the characters about all that this moment means. Behind and below are two shores, presumably the Holy Land and Egypt, facing each other. The towns from which the family has fled are blueish, as if under-water. The ones they are travelling towards are sunlit and clear. A falling tree and red flowers presage the Crucifixion; a white bird flies over the dark chasm ahead.

The painting is a small theatre of displacement, of the seen and the veiled, reminding us that asylum-seekers carry with them both a future and a past. Landscape, Bruegel lets us under-stand, is not only the context of our lives, the place where we enact life-changing moments, but also earth in active relation to the human. This is not the hostile planet faced by migrating birds but nature taking part in our history and in our own migrations.

The Wild One

(for Roy Foster)

She stands beside a death mask under a chandelier,
head turning from an unseen source of light.
She's holding a leather Thucydides
and a seventeenth-century trumpet
without piston, slide or valve
as if she doesn't know what to do with it
and might prefer a lute. On the map behind

South is torn from North, the West on top,
East nowhere. On the canvas, all that shows
are glaucous leaves of laurel for her hair.
The real picture, the one Vermeer never sold
even at his poorest, is himself – painting History
in disguise as a maenad. We might take her hand,
step her down from the frame,

dress her in jeans and a T-shirt, open those eyes.
She's not a scholar collating an archive
though she'll help if they're fair, nor a journalist
after a story, twisting what's said to make scandal,
sell. Though she's on their side too, if they mean well.
She's blood from the heart's right ventricle,
witness and balance, sift, record and judge.

Her name Clio comes from glory, telling
glorious things we did. But she's a wild one!
Look at her – making us feel out of depth
or guilty for not listening. Oh, she's foul play.
She's dust on a galactic nebula, nothing to do
with today. She'll spend centuries name-checked
and dismissed. *History's bunk*. But she's all there is.

> *Johannes Vermeer*, The Art of Painting
> (The Artist in his Studio) *(1666),*
> *Kunsthistorisches Museum, Vienna*

Homo ergaster *and the Red Horizon*

One move will betray us to predators
but in this pink haze, a mist so close
to the scorching ground it's almost solid,
are fingers chipping stone flakes

and something is splashing through streams
rising from a ridge where earthquake
has tilted the land, and Olduvai Gorge
has split into opposing cliffs.

There are five of them, look, silent as blown seed.
But they're being followed. All of them,
forerunners and pursuers, heading for the red
horizon, where cumulus burrs the soil

like dough of unleavened bread
which just might rise and ferment.
They're following the valley-bed
through the crewel-work of thorn on rock

past a gold flash of an estuary – ocean
seen for the first time – into the first new continent.
But we're stronger, we survive.
This is the winnowing, the winning out.

Stone strikes stone, shaping an axe
and a knife. Sparks fly into the night.
A soft gasp of fear, and surprise, fans the dark
isosceles bud of the first flame into life.

Riders from the East

Wheel. Axle. Chain. *These are the three sons*
of Noah. Of them was the earth o'erspread.
Breath of horses at night. I drink mare's milk
and eat foal flesh. I listen for hooves on the plain
and herd-swirl in cold starlight.

They went forth from Ur of the Chaldees –
artists of collapsible homes, learning to ride
in the Steppes: inventing the bit, inventing the rein.
Travelling was where we began. Yak, camel, boat . . .
Leaving on every trail the written sign for *wagon,*

adding a pebble to the cairns on the pack-path
towards the holy mountain; stringing bright flags
for the wind to carry our prayers
up over the misty pass and its guardians
to the realm of the Thunder Dragon.

Leaving Troy

You've given away your temple, Lord,
your altar-stone, dun flame of burning myrrh,
oil poured in long libations, soaking our turf,
smoke rising to your sky from incense-
sacrifices kindled by our grandfathers.
You've given away our holy mountain,
dipterocarp, deciduous, evergreen,
where wolf and panther pugmarks
print ivied ridge-trails, and cedars flush
in dawn's first light under snow.
You've betrayed all this
to our enemies, the Greeks.

I was on his boat. As we left, we saw
an old man – a fire-eater, deranged –
caper on the beach. The scorched hills
behind our charred walls
quivered through the dark part of his flame.
Our city was a scatter on the plain.
Old men and children
huddled round griddle-stones watching us go.
This was the shore where for ten years
they beached their carbony hulls
like a pod of orca, and sat by driftwood fires

like the thousand brightspeckle stars
of the Milky Way. This was the jetty

where they herded our women on board
at spear-point, and sailed away.

The prince couldn't take us all
and few, even now, would exchange
their wrecked home for this terrace
of salt in blue cellulite, green petals
dimpling on milk, a sheen like snow
cancelling its own shadow.
Me, I was OK up to Tenedos.
I'd gone there once with a girl, before
the enemy hid in the island's little bay
and we thought they'd gone.
It took a hard heart to leave
those inlets behind for the blazoned sea.

Light, scattered from a cereal packet.
Razzle like cameras at an audience of the Pope.
(Forgive me my clairvoyance.
Let's say I was a prophet, once.)

Then hammers of rain,
I remember, that first day. Our wake
was a greenish patina, a portal
to the undercounter world, gritty caverns
of nymphs, lamp eyes, blubbery warriors.
Jade on a flayed-steel prairie; fields of cream
on ocean-flesh soon dark in our first sunset.
No room for pity here: just red,

syncopated green. What lies ahead?
Charybdis, Scylla, Africa, civil war.
Take it or leave it, the bread we eat
was baked in the volcano of our city.

The Mission

(from Virgil, The Aeneid, *Book 4)*

Who could fool an obsessed lover? The woman ran
on absolute jitter anyway, even over little things,
and now was the first to realise they were leaving.

She trembled, break-steel rigid, furious. He and his boys
were fitting up the ships! She raged through the streets
like a maenad blooded by the god. 'Traitor! Did you
                                                  think

you'd slip off on the quiet? What about our love –
and the death I know I'll die here if you go?
Why scuttle across high seas in winter storms? If Troy

still stood, if you weren't flying into the unknown
to grab someone else's lands, would you rush headlong
into the waves? Is it me you're running from?

See these tears? There's nothing else left me, is there?
Think how we came together, the marriage we've begun.
If I've deserved anything, if any bit of me was dear

to you, give up this wild scheme and wild mood you're
                                                       in.
It's your fault my people and the Libyans hate me. Look
what I've earned for your sake – shame!

I called you *husband*. Now it's *guest* –
and you're leaving me to die? If only there'd been a child
to play in the palace courtyards and bring your face

                                                    back to me,

I wouldn't feel so used and so abandoned!'
He struggled not to meet her eyes.
He thought of the gods' warning. He tried

to quash all feeling in his heart. 'I can't deny
I owe you a million kindnesses. I won't forget.
I didn't plan to slip away in secret – don't think that!

But I didn't pretend to marry you, either.
That was never on the cards. If Fate had left me free
to follow what I love, I know where I'd be now –

rebuilding Troy, looking after my family.
I'd think of the defeated, the hell they went through
and put back Priam's roof. But I'm a refugee –

you know that – on a mission. God told me to take Italy
so Italy must be my country and my love. You're Asian
in a Libyan city: what's wrong with us Trojans

finding a place in the sun – in Europe? Don't we have a

                                                    right

to kingdom? Every night, as darkness wraps the earth
in shadow, and star-burn rises in black sky,

I see my father's ghost panicking, warning me
that by staying I defraud my own son of a future
in the west. But now the gods have sent, I swear,

a messenger. I saw him in plain daylight. The gods
have spoken! So, enough. Stop this hysterical
sobbing, torturing us both. I'm not going of my own
                                                    free will.'

The Appointment

Flamingo silk. New ruff, the ivory ghost of a halter.
Chestnut curls, commas behind the ear. 'Taller,
by half a head, than my Lord Walsingham.'

His Devon-cream brogue, malt eyes. New cloak
mussed in her mud. The Queen leans forward,
a rosy envelope of civet, a cleavage whispering
                                    seed-pearls.

Her own sleeve rubs that speck of dirt on his cheek.
Three thousand ornamental fruit baskets swing
in the smoke. 'It is our pleasure to have our servant
                                    trained

some longer time in Ireland.' Stamp out
marks of the Irish. Their saffron smocks.
All carroughs, bards and rhymers. Desmonds

and O'Donnells grin on low spikes, an avenue
of heads to the war tent. Kerry timber sold
to the Canary Isles. Pregnant girls

hung by their own hair on city walls. Then plague,
crumpling gargoyles through Munster. 'They spoke
like ghosts crying out of their graves.'

Kywash (On John White's Lost Colony)

'Master White, an excellent painter, carried very many
people into Virginia, there to inhabit.'

Forgive me. Even cats dream. When wind fans these
                                            Atlantic
mists apart, you, sir, may see wave-fleece breaking on
                                            Irish rocks.
But I see snow geese on Croatoan Island, melon-vine
lacing the sandbars, dogwood leaning from wild gusts
the other side of this same ocean, yes, the very same,
and yaupon berries red like holly here at Yule.

I see us arrive at Wococon that first time. The marsh
                                            grass
ruffling. Our first sight of them, fishing. A woman
seething meat in pots of earth, a child
moving logs under as they burned. I see myself
painting an old man smiling at me from his winter rug
and a mother with her child, at Pomeiooc.

Their sitting at meat: a husband and his wife,
smiling at me and at each other. I painted Secoton
village in its muffler of pumpkins and corn.
The Charnel House, where they preserve each
                                            werowance.
There they lie for eternity, side by side, their flesh
removed, their skin replaced and stuffed with leather,

black topknots on their heads, watched over by their

                                                    idol,

mysterious Kywash. How do *we* keep those we have

                                                    lost?

At the summer feast, I painted their circle-dance,
intricacies of tattoo on shifting muscle. We dreamed
a fortune, too. Of course we did. We'd traded
one copper plate for fifty skins. They were welcoming,

they taught us how to live: to open clams dropped by

                                                    gulls,

pluck bayberries to make candles. Then the Governor's
silver cup went missing and we burned
the village of Aquascogoc. I came back to a lost place
in the temple: my dear wife had passed. But the child

                                                    was fine

and the man I chose for her was good. Amen to that.

The second time, we came with women – and one of

                                                    them

my girl. I watched her child grow inside her
through the three-month voyage. From the Sound,
we saw our ramparts down. Deer
grazed the vine on our roofless huts. We stumbled on
one broke-up skeleton – a man we'd left, but who?

My brave girl: first sight of this new world
and she was near her time. Then we lost a fellow
shot in the surf by an arrow. In punishment

I burned their village. I would to God
men could undo what they have done.
In August she bore her child, Virginia.

If I could hear her voice, I'd die a happy man.
But it was me they chose – they entreated me – to go
back for supplies. That was the only hour I saw her cry.
I touched her temple, soft as the baby's head,
and rowed out to the boat. Now look at me,
the father who came three years too late.

My third time, the water was boiling round the rocks.
I found the fort deserted, chests I'd hid dug up.
But no sign of distress. And the code we agreed
was part-carved on a tree. I tell this for her sake.
They journeyed on without me. This I know.
They're deep now, deep in the mainland. Safe.

John White, Watercolours of America *(1585)*,
British Museum, London

Directions for the Plantation
of Ulster, 1610

'We go with thirteen squires. Richard Hare
of Suffolk, income fifty pounds per annum,
has the papers. You're a lucky man to get on the roll.
The softer Worcester lot prefer Armagh
and lay their orchards out like dreams of the Vale
of Evesham. We clear the land of rock
then break it, keeping caliver and musket primed
in the last furrow, against black trees.

We build turrets of local granite, throw up wattle
                                                                bothies
for our tenants, track the human wolves unto their lairs
and terminate. A pleasant sport – and fair prey falls
to the followers.' So wrote Thos Blennerhasset,
Norfolk squire, dedicating his pamphlet
to the youngest British prince
and smiling like one of his sponsored angels, carved
on lime-wood rafters in the village church back home.

The Colossus

A naked giant, fist raised, eyes closed,
cut off at the hips by the skyline, strides
across the land, buttocks swaddled
in black smoke. He's backdrop to our lives
and dwarfs the lot of us. We're incidental.
Wherever he's from, he's heading for beyond.
In the valley, villagers pour away.
You've never seen cows run like this
or riders fall. Only one thing stands still
among hurtling refugees. A donkey –

bemused or shocked; or bloody-minded
and just not going to budge. Maybe deaf
and it hasn't looked behind as the giant thuds,
flattening God knows what
beneath his feet, revving the blaze
of his torso, a swish of rage
out of any scale we knew about,
invisible loins feeding their own mad dream.
Will you kiss its hand? Where will it stop?
How did it stomp so easily into our home?

Francisco de Goya, The Colossus *(1808–12),*
Museo del Prado, Madrid

Landscape with Flight into Egypt

Here we are in mountains, at a pass
between two shadows, before we descend
the black path. Against the gleam of an inlet
fretted with tow-coloured towns, a black tree

splinters and falls to an upside-down cross.
An idol slips out of a shrine and above the gulf
a hooded crow sits on a leafless stump.
Landscape is your life seen in distance, when you know

for just an interval of sunlight, how to join
time travelled with time still to go.
We have passed a red scatter of anemones
with no fore-memory of blood. Before us and behind

are cities, all that sweet clustering of 'civilised'.
In one, the massacre we're running from.
The other is asylum. I can't see your eyes
and you can't see mine, but a white bird flies

across this chasm we have to go down into.
It's us and the child. Home is the journey.
Home is the wild, with no one to share it,
no one to stand and gaze

at pale light falling on arches, alleyways
and ziggurats clenched in their own lives
like crowds dancing in a street outside
while the Lover, the wild Singer, dies.

Pieter Bruegel the Elder, Landscape with
Flight into Egypt *(1563)*, *Courtauld
Gallery, London*

Strangers

In the nineteenth century a new country rose like a new moon for refugees from all over the world, a home for the homeless, celebrated in lines written by the Jewish-American poet Emma Lazarus in 1883 and inscribed below the Statue of Liberty:

> Give me your tired, your poor,
> Your huddled masses yearning to breathe free,
> The wretched refuse of your teeming shore.
> Send these, the homeless, tempest-tost to me.

Here was a nation created by migration. A society of immigrants, as John F. Kennedy called it long after: 'A nation of people with the fresh memory of old traditions, who dare to explore new frontiers.'

Immigration into America, and migration west within it to find new land, was happening long before the Statue of Liberty arrived. If one could have looked down from a satellite on Russia and

America in the middle of the nineteenth century you would have seen two streams of similar wagons crawling across the two huge continents in opposite directions.

The Russians making for the wild east of Siberia were escaping the feudal system of the Tsars, hoping for land and dreaming of fortunes to be made in mining and furs. The new Americans, inching west, were escaping poverty and likewise hoping for land, gold, fortune, work and a new and better life.

In 2003 in Siberia I met the descendants of native peoples whose land the Russian pioneers had taken in the 1860s. The grandmother of Olga, the woman who escorted us into the forest, had been born in one of those pioneer wagons. In an area set apart as a reservation and a museum for the tribes who once lived by fishing along the Amur River, Olga introduced us to the Nanai, whose land her forebears had taken.

Until Ellis Island was enlarged by landfill from the New York subway and a processing facility built, immigrants to America arrived at several different landing-points. When Ellis Island opened its doors to immigrants in January 1892, first through was a fifteen-year-old Irish girl. Twelve million followed. In the peak year, 1907, it was a million and a quarter.

For the indigenous tribes, one focus of resistance was the railroad. The 1962 film *How the West Was Won* follows four generations of an American family moving west from the 1830s. They are first attacked by Cheyenne Indians; then a railroad company violates a treaty by building on the territory of the Arapaho Indians, who retaliate by stampeding buffalo through the camp. The railroads opened the land to the settlers, they unified and connected, but whatever joins can also separate and the railroads became a symbol of loneliness. The blues of Robert Johnson (born in 1911 in Mississippi, when slavery had been abolished but its legacy remained) spoke for all railroad workers in the Delta, and his songs echoed among later African Americans leaving the South for Chicago:

> The train it left the station with two lights on behind.
> Well the blue light was my blues and the red light was
> my mind.

Migration builds civilisation. But as civilisation grows, it also causes displacement and fragmentation. In Europe, the Industrial Revolution had winners and losers, creating massive emigration across frontiers and seas, and also inside each country. In America, one railroad theme was the way it took people away from those they loved. 'I was riding Number 9, heading south from Caroline,' sang Hank Williams, born in 1923, the frail son of a railroad worker. 'Left my gal and left my home. I heard that lonesome whistle blow.'

In the twentieth century emigration became the quintessential experience of our time, and a key self-image was the human being unhoused, like Beckett's tramp heroes or Brecht's Mother Courage. And one of the most famous twentieth-century American photographs was 'Migrant Mother'.

During the Great Depression the photographer Dorothea Lange was working for the Farm Security Administration in California. In March 1936 she came to a camp of migrant workers devastated because the crops they had come to pick had been destroyed by freezing rain. She took six photographs of Florence Thompson with her children in their canvas shelter, telling her these pictures would help people in other camps. Florence had left Oklahoma in 1926 for California. Her husband died, leaving her pregnant, and with five children to feed. With another partner and a growing family she joined the thousands of victims of the Depression streaming into California in old cars and trucks from the Midwest, Arkansas, Kansas, Texas and Oklahoma.

Lange gave the photos to the Resettlement Administration in Washington, which sent 20,000 pounds of food to migrant camps. (Migrant was the polite word; residents called them Okies.) But Lange also gave the photos to the Press. The *San Francisco News* published one of Florence which became known as 'Migrant Mother'. 'A migrant agricultural worker's family,' ran the caption. 'Seven hungry children.'

Long after, in the 1970s, Florence wrote to a local newspaper, 'I wish she hadn't taken my picture. I can't get a penny out of it. She didn't ask my name. She said she wouldn't sell the pictures. She said she'd send me a copy. She never did.' In 1983 Florence got cancer and had a stroke. Her children couldn't afford nursing care and gave her story to the *San Jose Mercury News*. The story and picture made national headlines. Two thousand letters, and $35,000 in crumpled bills, poured from all over the United States into a Migrant Mother Fund administered by the Hospice Caring Project of Santa Cruz County.

'The famous picture of your mother for years gave me great strength, pride and dignity because she exuded those qualities so,' wrote a woman from Santa Clara. 'Enclosed is a check for $10 to assist the woman whose face gave and still gives eloquent expression to the need our country has not met,' said a note from New York.

'None of us understood how deeply Mama's photo affected people,' said Florence's son. 'The photo had always been a bit of a curse. After those letters it gave us a sense of pride.'

But there's a twist here that touches on all questions of 'migration' and 'native', all the 'where-are-you-froms?' Florence, born Florence Leona Christie in 1903, was a full-blooded Cherokee. She was born in a tepee on an Indian reservation, descendant of the forced migrations known as the Trail of Tears. Her ancestors had come to Oklahoma a hundred years before, when the Indian Removal Act of 1830 forced Native Americans out of their southern homelands. The Choctaw had already gone, giving up their homeland by treaty. Their chief told the *Arkansas Gazette* the migration was a 'trail of tears and death'. The Seminole were shifted by force. Four years later the Cherokee followed: 4,000 out of 15,000 died from exposure and starvation on the way. By 1883, 46,000 Native Americans had been forced from their homes in the south-east states, leaving 25 million acres for European settlers.

Florence died aged eighty. Her tombstone reads: *Migrant Mother – a Legend of the Strength of American Motherhood*. By a stroke of the mad muse of history, a Cherokee woman whose family was displaced by white America became the icon of American motherhood.

Blossom is browning and fading on the grass. The parakeets have not stopped the goldfinches breeding. We see very busy goldfinches every day: there must be at least two nests near. And we have found a house we might move to, if we manage to sell this one. Everywhere I go, I keep thinking of what has to be dismantled, left behind and got rid of, such as furniture and books, to fit into a smaller house; and wondering what plants I can take. Migration means leaving things behind. It moves you into a disoriented world which doesn't add up in the way you are used to. You have to start putting things together in a new way.

⁂

Without a home, everything is fragments. In the twentieth century, the 'chaff' produced by war and violent economic changes blew through the inhabited continents in stories of migration even more varied and dangerous than those of animals and birds. But migration also creates songs. Music unifies. Orpheus drew together rocks, trees, animals and people; songs connect the disconnected. Italian migrant workers remembering the railway stations where they parted from their families, sailors singing shanties at sea, slaves singing spirituals in the Delta, the Irish and Scots in America – all these songs reach back to a lost home, uniting singer and listeners with a place and people left behind. From 'Loch Lomond' and 'Shenandoah' to Hank Williams's 'Lonesome Whistle', songs of exile are a vital part of the music of every diaspora.

⁂

The Greek word for exile is *xeniteia*. Monks of late antiquity, yearning for spiritual detachment from society and remembering Genesis 12:1, 'Get you out of your land, your kindred and your father's home unto a land that I will show you', used it to mean 'alienation'; a 'being foreign' at the spiritual level they desired. But to nineteenth- and twentieth-century Greeks, *xeniteia* meant *having* to be away. *Xeniteia* was exile and pain; it was a longing for home that could not be assuaged by getting there, because you'll have to leave again.

This Greek diaspora was made of many social layers, ship-owners, sailors, merchants, metalworkers. They went not only to America and Australia but western and eastern Europe, the Danube Delta, the subcontinent and the Levant – wherever there was cloth or metal to be worked and carried elsewhere by an expanding fleet of merchant ships. Meanwhile, many Greeks came to Greek cities for work, missing their island homes. For all of them, the great note in their songs was longing for a home the singer could not live in; estrangement, both from that home and from whatever new place he had come to. It was the same hurt, angry mix of love and alienation from what you love which powered Argentinian tango, Portuguese fado and the blues. This is what the Greeks associated with *xeniteia*, whose basic meaning is 'being strange'. It comes from the Ancient Greek *xenos*, 'stranger', from which we also get that word (which reminds us that *alienus* is a name for the devil) 'xenophobia'.

But in the earliest recorded Greek, *xenos* meant not only 'stranger' but 'guest-friend'. This was a pivotal relationship in an ancient culture which knew that when you were travelling you needed protection. A network of reciprocal 'guest friend-ship' spread across the archaic Greek world. *When you come, I will look after you. Make yourself home in my home.* Homeric hosts give their guests rich presents on departure.

The rules of generosity, hospitality and its obligations were often abused, of course. But they *were* the rules: *xenos* was the basis of the system underlying social relations.

Helping strangers was an obligation in ancient Judaism, too. If you look up the word 'foreigner' in the Bible, you find many exhortations to help the stranger. 'If any of your fellow Israelites become poor and are unable to support themselves,' orders Leviticus, 'help them as you would help a foreigner and stranger.' 'I was a father to the needy, I took up the case of the stranger,' says Job. 'No stranger had to spend the night in the street; my door was always open to the traveller.' 'Do not forget to show hospitality to strangers,' Paul reminds the Hebrews.

Despite the pogroms and anti-Semitism that were to scar Europe later, built into her most ancient language and also her most ancient faith is the obligation of generosity between host and guest, resident and migrant.

There are hundreds of diasporas all over the world, but as birds are the blueprint for migration so are the Jews for diaspora and exile.

In the seventeenth century BC, famine forced the Israelites to migrate to Egypt. In the thirteenth century, Moses led them out of Egypt, and after forty years of wandering Joshua led them in to the Promised Land. In 586 BC Jerusalem and the First

Temple were destroyed and the Jews were exiled to Babylon. Many came back fifty years later when the Persians overthrew Babylon, but in AD 70 the Romans destroyed the Second Temple and the Jews were scattered, and often persecuted, over the globe.

In March 1938, when Hitler entered Vienna, even the author of *Civilisation and Its Discontents* found himself at risk from persecution. Sigmund Freud was eighty-two and in constant pain from mouth cancer. He had lived and worked in the same flat since 1891 and was reluctant to leave. He hoped fame would protect him. But the Nazis kept his home under surveillance, fixed a swastika to the building, sent storm troopers to invade the flat and interrogated his daughter. When Freud was invited to England, friends advanced the money the Nazis demanded (they called it income tax) and secured him safe passage. With his wife, daughter and dog, Freud left for London. Five months later came Kristallnacht, the Night of Broken Glass and the beginning of Hitler's Final Solution. Ninety-five synagogues in the city were destroyed; fifteen hundred throughout Austria. Thirty thousand Jews were taken to concentration camps. His four sisters died in the camps.

People from other religions projected on to their own situations the plight of the Jews in Babylon, in bondage in Egypt, or in the wilderness.

When Protestantism was banned in France, French Huguenots fled to (among other places) the Cévennes. Pastors preached secretly on mountaintops and women carried portable altars hidden under their skirts. They called this period of the sixteenth and seventeenth centuries Le Désert, after the years the Jews spent in the wilderness. African American slaves in the southern states of nineteenth-century America identified with the Jews hoping under Joshua's leadership to reach the Promised Land. The Ohio River was Jordan – they sang of home, sweet Canaan, and the free country across the Jordan. *One more river, and that's the river of Jordan. One more river, there's one more river to cross.* In 1998 the Dalai Lama, before he was awarded the Nobel Peace Prize, asked Jewish leaders what their secret was. Tibetans, he said, admired the Jews because 'no matter how they are scattered through all corners of the earth, they maintained their sense of unity of the people'. How had they done this through 1,900 years of diaspora? The rabbis explained that in Jewish observance the centre of cultural and religious identity is the family home. This is what replaced the destroyed Temple. All over Europe, North Africa and Asia, lighting candles in the home on Friday night, saying prayers which bless domestic tasks and welcoming the Sabbath in under your own roof, countered the estrangement and displacement of exile.

Jewish exile and longing for the Promised Land also became a Christian image of spiritual alienation: of the longing to return (after the Fall) to a right relationship with God. In 1843 a British Christian who felt Palestine should be given to the Jewish people spoke of 'a land without a people for a people without a land', a phrase which ricocheted through Middle East politics and in the twentieth century was taken to express a mistaken Zionist belief that the land was empty of inhabitants before the settlers got there. And so, eventually, reversing one exile created another. The refugees became the new Colossus.

After modern Israel was founded, its first great fiction writer was Yizhar Smilansky, whose pen name was S. Yizhar. Yizhar's parents were Russian immigrants to Ottoman Palestine, where he was born in 1916. In his autobiographical novel *Preliminaries* he describes what it was like for his parents working this supposedly empty land. His father sees it in animal – but also Biblical – terms as 'a place of snakes and scorpions'. The baby nearly dies of stings because the father, ignorant of the indigenous fauna, leaves it on a wasp nest while he ploughs. Is this the promised land? Maybe, thinks the father, driving his son across the desert scrub to a doctor, 'it was a fundamental mistake. Maybe this land doesn't want us at all.' The mother sees it in human terms. 'Who knew about the Arabs where she came from? Nobody talked about them back in the Volhynian forest on the bank of the River Styr.'

In his novella *Kirbet Khizeh*, as controversial when it appeared in 1949 as it is today, yet still on the Israeli school curriculum, Yizhar drew on his experience as an intelligence officer from 1946 to 1948 to describe the clearance of Arab villages. Young Israeli soldiers capture a peaceful Arab village and load villagers into trucks at gunpoint. Aren't they allowed belongings or water? asks the driver. 'No,' he is told. 'Take them away from here, let them go to hell.' The soldiers ease their conscience by saying these people are 'like animals'. When the narrator voices moral qualms, the others say 'stop thinking so much'.

The parents of the Palestinian poet Mahmoud Darwish lived in a village called Birwe in the district of Akka (Acre, to the Crusaders) in Upper Galilee. When he was six, Israeli soldiers attacked his village. The family joined 900,000 other Palestinians fleeing the possibility of massacre and became refugees in Lebanon. When they returned 'illegally' to their village in 1949 it had been cleared of Arabs like Yizhar's fictional Kirbet Khizeh, rebuilt and colonised by Jews. Four hundred other villages suffered the same fate. The family settled in Galilee too late to count as Arab Israelis, so they were denied Israeli nationality. Unable to travel in their own country without Israeli permission, they now had a new identity as illegal 'infiltrators', 'present-absent aliens'. They were internal refugees.

No poet is a stranger to estrangement. Many write out of their relationship to home but this relationship changes through a working life and some write out of a sense of *not* belonging. In a poem called 'Exposure', written when he was migrating from conflicted Northern Ireland to the Republic of Ireland, Seamus Heaney uses the phrase 'inner émigré' for his relation to the land where he grew up. The poem portrays the poet leaving his troubled homeland as a 'woodkerne escaped from the massacre', and invokes two other poet exiles, Gerard Manley Hopkins and the Russian poet Osip Mandelstam.

For Hopkins, an English priest posted to Dublin, Ireland itself was exile. His sonnet 'To Seem a Stranger' voices his estrangement 'in Ireland . . . at a third/ Remove.' Mandelstam was sent into internal exile by Stalin in the 1930s. In 1938 he was again accused of anti-Soviet views and sentenced to Siberia, where he died. Heaney describes Mandelstam as a man who deliberately travelled light; for whom the prospect of exile 'was not altogether disabling'.

Elizabeth Bishop's aesthetic was inseparable from her travels away from home. Her collections are titled *North and South*, *Questions of Travel*, *Geography III* – just as those of the Greek poet George Seferis, through the Second World War, are *Log Book I, II* and *III*, as if his poems are notes from one voyage of exile.

The poet Ramsey Nasr was born in Rotterdam, but his father came from Salfit on the West Bank – where, in 1978, soldiers took away his fields and built Israel's largest settlement, Ariel. The town has 45,000 people. There is now a wall through it to protect the settlers against the land's original owners, like the Ulster settlers of 1611 protecting themselves against the woodkerne.

Thirty-three years later, as the Knesset passed the draft of a law directing Palestinians to pay the costs of demolishing their own homes, Israeli soldiers took over the land of a Palestinian man with heart disease. They prevented him from stepping on it, declared it a closed military area and pulled up his 300 olive trees.

'When you are displaced,' says another Palestinian poet, Mourid Barghouti, who, as a student in Egypt during the Six Days War suddenly became a permanent exile from his home town of Ramallah, 'every home you have is the home of others too.'

During the Israeli invasion of Lebanon in 2006 I was in Madrid. My daughter was working there and I took my mother to visit her. In the Prado, the first thing that hit us was Bruegel's *The Triumph of Death*, painted in 1562 (around the same time as

Landscape with the Fall of Icarus), while the Spanish persecution of Protestants was getting worse. Not until Goya painted *Disasters of War*, 250 years later, did European art depict war at this pitch. Pictures of Lebanon that night on TV struck the same chord.

Migrant Mother

They are Okies, pea-pickers brought to ground
by a skanky engine, crawling through the Land
of Promise like her grandma up the Trail of Tears
a hundred years before. In the lens, they're a study
in achromatic grey. *Yes, you may take my picture.*
Freeze-dust, an hour-after-hour glass, spun
by the Witch of the East and blown through
a workless morning in spiralling wind.

Just one freak frost. They're screwed,
the battered pea-vines say so. Those that can leave
have left. *Count yourself lucky if you find
rope for the canvas, a real floor
under your feet.* Seven hungry children.
Folk selling their tents for food.

The Letter Home

(for Gieve Patel)

You painted the Saturday queue
for a Letter Writer cross-legged on a shawl
in shadow of the unfinished flyover. *I have health,*
again and again. *I am sending the money home.*
But what is home? Where you began,
where a sister – with a husband whose salary is regular
but he resents you anyway, this indigent
who sees more of the world than he – has turned
your family against you while you are gone –
or where the journeys take you: where work is
when you sleep behind plastic, tacked
to urinous breeze block, and cook at the edge
of a five-lane you are helping to build
watched by ashy-necked crows who make their nests
out of sanitary towels from mounds of trash to the east?

We are breaking stone for the motorway.
I will come home when work is done.

Under the luminous fuzz that does for stars in this city
you look into the well, wondering where it went wrong,
what you could have done better. Look up.
The hurt sky is bandaged in cloud,
earth has reversed her magnetic field
and the Mumbai monsoon, blown sideways

like glycerine skirts, has calmed the grit
that gets everywhere into wetsilk paintable gleams
reminding us where it has come from, this element
we all desire and have to struggle with. Home.
The round white pebble with a blue-cut heart.
Whole geological dowries
of copper, hooded turquoise, amethyst.

Mumbai, July–November 2010

What You Told Me about Islands

(i.m. Kay Cicellis and Nikos Palaiologos)

1 The Two Flames

Let's say you found each other like repeating flames
in an antique mirror, trailing the memory
of two Greek ports in foreign lands
where you were born, and two islands
you fled back to when the devil began to dance
in mad *Evropi* and you learned the island song
of eternal *ritornelle:* one hotgold summer
when you find yourself, then rage to get away,
darkwinter alcohol, high winds to cut you off,
a closed-in grey horizon and a harbour
where all your debts and fantasies are known;
while beyond the mountain one small bay
waits on: never not dreamed of, life-long
loved – and left. The soul's a wanderer and fugitive,
driven by decrees and laws of gods.

2 *Blown Ruby*

As if they were itinerant stained-glass makers
setting up camp outside a mediaeval town
at the edge of forest, or here in Athens by *Plinteria*
ti Merimna, even as we speak, or on the island

at the corner of Ayias Annas and Spiridonos,
they're lighting their transformation fires to conjure
                                                        glass
from wood and sand. Bellows. Three furnaces
for heating, cooling, melting. *Cristallo*, azurite,

blown ruby. They come, villagers would say,
they speak in foreign languages, and when they go
our windows are alive with coloured light.
By the fire at night you'd hear their stories

of other worlds they brought to life in glass.
Slow campfire melting. Tools, barter, trade.
Sun scatters, uneven as heartbreak,
through imperfections in everything they made.

You transform *us* we'd say, in welcome.
They will not come again. Close your eyes.
A branch is being broken
and the soot-bruised earth is warm.

Athens 2005

The Music of Home

(for Nikos Daskalakis)

Arriving at Ellis Island, I watch the glass alps of
$\qquad\qquad\qquad\qquad$ Manhattan soar
above one-storey buildings
that must have looked terrifying when they were the
$\qquad\qquad\qquad\qquad\qquad$ only ones
as you came over the rainbow from Europe in 1854 . . .
Yes, soar, and take off from the emerald of Battery Park
like vagrant emperor dragonflies beginning their long
migrate across the Indian Ocean. Arriving at Ellis Island
(hoisted on landfill from bowels of the New York
$\qquad\qquad\qquad\qquad\qquad\qquad$ subway
on a knoll once private to fishermen and gulls),
I head for treasures donated by families
whose great-great-grandparents manhandled them
all of three thousand miles. 'She took all she could
$\qquad\qquad\qquad\qquad\qquad\qquad$ carry,'
fathers reminded children in a thousand languages.

How about we go there Niko, someday? You'd get up
from your apartment in Heraklion where your daughter
is at music college and where, before you were so ill, I
$\qquad\qquad\qquad\qquad\qquad$ heard her sing
under the old walls which used, as I recall, to shelter a
$\qquad\qquad\qquad\qquad\qquad\qquad$ bar
hollowed out from Saracen stone

where we'd swig home-stilled raki and dance on
sawdust
while an old man sang the *Erotokritos*
and played spoons on his knee. The moat is cleaned up
now,
paved and re-hewn for family recreation.
Yes, arriving at Ellis Island, you and I,
we'd begin with a Finnish copper coffee pot,
a panel of embroidered silk from China, a mould
for rice crackers (Japan), a Turkish towel from Palestine,

a brass noodle-cutter from Austro-Hungary like two
linked raincoloured spurs, and a carved coconut
from Guyana. But then we'd light on the Armenian 'oud
and Hungarian zither, the horsehair bow from Korea,
the Irish tambourine and finally the little Cretan lyra
complete with its bow of hawk bells
like the lyra played by Thanassis Skordalos
on his first recording, 1946, with Giannis
Markogiannakis on lute. And we'd remind each other
how we used to work all day in the burning sun
then dance all night. How Kostas, aged seventy,
showed us the steps of Pentozali but we could never
keep up with the flicker of his neat black shoes.

And we'd laugh, that dancing and singing to lyra
mattered more in the dark, on Ariadne's shore,
than anything on earth. Arriving alone today
at Ellis Island I think of the years you worked

the boats. Your letters came rarely because your hand,
you said after, was never steady. One ship
anchored you a year off Egypt, a national scandal
hushed up, two hundred Greek cement vessels
dead in one enormous harbour –
no one had paid anyone, it was a combat zone
for dodgy insurance companies with you
in the middle, you never got your wages
and had to pawn your underpants to get repatriated –

but one velvet night you heard Cretan music
over the water and next day you dived
into that swamp of sewage, sharks and garbage thrown
from a thousand ships, as into an avenue
of green silk, to find the one guy
in this madhouse playing the music of home.

Music from the Deep

(for Nicholas de Lange)

Clio? I met her in the synagogue of the Mellah
behind the gun of the Moroccan security guard
who asked for our ID. East and west
changed place up there among the headscarves
of the women's quarters, looking down
on pews of men with *tefillin*
strapped to their foreheads and biceps.

Hearing the Book of Esther read at Purim,
in Hebrew, was like listening online
to music from a deep-sea crustal plate.
She introduced me, your Clio, to the system
of imaginaries – like checking the atomic weight
of a syllable under a microscope
or embracing algebra as the science of pure time.

The Two-handled Jug

A stork is flying low
above an acre of graves
wrapped in pink dust

and protected by pink walls
where the storks nest.
This is the Jewish cemetery

Marrakesh. Scimitar wings
of the swallows, blue
calligraphy on blue. Plague tombs

of the fifteenth century.
Husbands, children, wives:
and bronze epigraphs

in French, Arabic, Hebrew.
Wearing a *yarmulkah* lent
by the caretaker, you decode

the names. I join you at the exit
where you wash your hands
in a cracked marble basin.

From a copper jug
you pour water, glass blossom,
through my fingers too.

The Freud Museum

It's 1938. Here's moss on red brick
at Nutley Terrace and an old man displaced,
just not too late, by swastikas on the portico
in Vienna. His daughter has been caretaking
their flight. The trunks hold a red-topped desk,
T'ang camel, phials of Etruscan glass
dug up from tombs, a print of the Pharoahs
at Abu Simbel and a red-lozenge Persian rug.
What is an object?
Shards from a lost world, gone to ground
then brought to light. *And home?* A sleeping child.
A nick-of-time railway pass. A letting-go
of neighbourhood gone wild.
Breath on the mirror. A dog, a garden. Found.

Freud Museum, London, 2011

Entry of the Sabbath

Only half-heard, the autumn
smoke of a viola blows
through the orchestra.

Far off, a blackbird
calls from that ancient temple
in the hazel grove.

Friday. Sunset.
A man lights two candles, alone,
and under his breath

intones a prayer
for love never possessed
too deep to say aloud.

Godfearing

We listened for the ringing of a bell
and catnapped between electric muezzin calls.
One of us got a photo of a mirage on the asphalt
over Ur – the very spot, they said, where Abraham

set out into the Talmud, into the Qu'ran
and then into small Saxon churches
and the sixty-foot Bleeding Heart, dripping neon
in Tennessee. They've named a war

after a racehorse and sent us to the desert
to interview a pilot
in chocolate-chip uniform. A brave boy
briefed to avoid mosques and never gloat.

How did he feel, making the first score
when he turned another plane
to a comet-hair fireball? With a man
like himself in there, who had a family, like him?

The difference, he guesses, *is the country
you come from. On the right side. Godfearing.*

London, 1990

Pieter the Funny One

Paint us, they said, the world as it is. No more
of your children's games and peasant weddings.
He painted *Procession to Calvary*, Saul
blasted by glory on the way to Damascus.

At home, now, transposing Holy Land to his own
familiar yellows, he did *Adoration of the Kings*
in snow. He was good at snow. Go on
they said. He did *Flight into Egypt*,

a *Census at Bethlehem*, branchy veins
down a red hound's legs.
Not one was satisfied. He made smoke
like dry ice lift over a bust chandelier

in rubble just that shade of dun
we see night after night on TV
in a totally annihilated village.
There are bodies in there you can't see,

he said. Forty disabled kids
with their mothers. And a Beirut reporter.
That's more like it, they said. We want
the world we live in. He painted *Slaughter*

of the Innocents (putting them, too, in snow)
and three hundred thousand refugees
in a red-and-black landscape.
Not hell, but it could have been.

From a plasma screen
he painted a boy of twelve,
his mouth that open-mouth mask
of Tragedy, plastered crimson

head to toe, standing over
his mother's living torso;
her arms taken off by bomb-blast
on the way to Damascus.

He conjured the home of the Caliphs
in flames like orange lilies – thrown
by an emperor whose religion
was founded on mercy –

and a game-show host from Nebraska
upset the President of Iraq didn't get
that Israel had a right to defend itself.
(By now the boy's mother had died.)

He started a new thing, skeletons
knifing a king,
another side-saddle on a grey horse
in the shafts of a broke-wheeled caboose

laden with bodies; a lone corpse
floating, swelled belly upwards,
downriver, dogs gnawing the face
of a toddler: plus three-headed Cerberus,

one head searching for fleas, one head
asleep, the third keeping watch
on a black bird making its nest
in red jasmine. They praised

the painstaking draughtsmanship
in his torn men dying on wheels,
failed rebels stuck on poles
in a cassis-coloured sky

and black plumes on a high thin horizon
from cities on fire: including
I may say Nazareth. And Bethlehem
where the emperor's pin-up,

a.k.a. the Prince of Peace, was born.
He said that's what I've seen. Yes,
they said, that's what we wanted.
The Triumph of Death.

Madrid, 2006

Sphinxes on Thames

An obelisk set in Egyptian sands, 1460 BC,
winched vertical beside this khaki river
and inscribed with names of volunteers
who died in barge-boat *Cleopatra*, towing
a granite rocket through the Bay of Biscay.
Michael Burns, James Gardiner, William Patan,
Joseph Benton, William Askin.
Why yearn for the faraway monument
from someone else's home? A riddle
for Pharaoh Thotmes III – and these two
cat-calm Victorian lookalikes
on the bank, one shrapnel-pocked
by London's first air raid and both dreaming,
dreaming of Giza.

               What we've done comes back to us.
Lies told upriver in a Parliament; a war declared;
Michael Burns sent east again. The faraway
ignites in London. What moves
on four legs in the morning, two at noon
and three with the gathering twilight? At Victoria
bus routes are blocked for bomb alerts.
Gas canisters and cellphones wait in cars
outside a nightclub. A burning jeep
crashes the airport door while doctors,
trained in Bangalore, lay bombs
in the nearby hospital carpark. Scan

every city, jittery along its arteries.
Violence returns to violence
and the answer to the riddle, always, Man.

London–Glasgow, 2007

The Broken Mirror

A man met a lemming on a mountain path.

'What I've always wanted to ask,' he said, 'is why when you migrate, you all jump off a cliff into the sea.'

'What *I've* always wanted to know,' said the lemming, 'is why you don't.'

It's late May, my daughter is back from Bogotá, we have cleared out the garden shed and attic, got rid of a thousand books, and moved. I've spent the last month taking cardboard boxes to the dump, but yesterday we went to a ceremony in Keats House. They were planting a new plum tree in the spot where one stood in May 1819, when the house belonged to Charles Brown. The previous December, when the brother of his friend John Keats died, Brown had invited the 23-year-old poet to stay with him in Hampstead. Keats had arrived in shock and grief; now he had become fascinated by the song of a nightingale nesting in the garden. One morning, Brown said:

he took his chair from the breakfast-table to the grass-plot under a plum-tree, where he sat for two or three hours. When he came into the house, I perceived he had some scraps of paper in his hand, and these he was quietly thrusting behind the books. On inquiry, I found those scraps, four or five in number, contained his poetic feelings on the song of our nightingale.

Brown said it was he who rescued those scraps of paper, that he helped Keats put them together and 'Ode to a Nightingale' was born.

You can rescue a masterpiece, you can plant a new plum tree, but you won't catch nightingales nesting around here any more. Since 1994 they have declined in Britain by 60 per cent. They winter south of the Sahara and we have made the air they fly through and the land they fly over far more dangerous and inhospitable.

In the last five years there has been a drastic fall in the numbers of long-distance migrant birds coming to Britain. The lesser spotted woodpecker has declined by 59 per cent: tree pipits and spotted flycatchers by 70 per cent, cuckoos by 37 per cent since 1995. In 2007, scientists recorded 16 million swifts flying from Africa to Britain. Sixteen million exhausting journeys sounds a lot, but the numbers are nothing compared to what they used to be: swifts have gone down 40 per cent since 1994.

Every twenty minutes another animal or plant disappears. Ever since we discovered fire we have been changing the earth as it was formed in the late Devonian era by the first tree,

Archaeopteris. Since 1945 our population has more than doubled. Using up more of the planet we share with animals, driving them to extinction faster than new species can evolve, we live today in the midst of a great dying. The habitats in which animals have evolved to exist disappear as we expand and industrialise more of the globe. In Flatford Mill in Norfolk the summer air was thick with swallows twenty years ago. This year there's one nest. 'Not enough insects,' a birdwatcher told me. 'We've been too successful in eliminating insects. There's simply not enough for the swallows to eat.'

A few years ago, in the Natural History Museum's Old Store Room, I wandered through chill corridors of staring animal heads, past carefully made glass eyes fitted into the heads of deer which no longer exist.

A village called Al-Qurnah stands today where the Tigris and Euphrates flow together to make a river known as Shatt al-Arab. This river flows on into the Persian Gulf but is drying up now, polluted by human activity.

Many say this was the original site of the Garden of Eden. The villagers of Al-Qurnah identify one tree on the bank as the Tree of Life.

We are the Colossus now.

Migrant birds are particularly at risk from the way we have changed and are changing the planet, for they have to negotiate so many different habitats and we are altering them all. Birds adapt quickly to change because their lives and species depend on it and today, with the changing climate, many have already altered their patterns of migration. With rising temperatures in spring and summer, some long-distance migrants have shifted their breeding ranges north. But this lengthens their spring journey and as the Sahara creeps south their autumn journey will lengthen, too. So fewer of them make it and their numbers thin. Thousands of other birds are also sliced up by wind farms just as geese stopping for a rest are trapped in oily rivers.

Other migrating species are affected too. Indian elephants are hit by trains running across their migration corridors; global warming is changing the places and food sources on which marine as well as aerial migrants depend. The Arctic is no longer the place to which thousands of creatures evolved to go in summer. Naturalists live with the nightmare that one year the migrants won't show up at all.

———

We are like but also unlike the nature which surrounds us. Animals use magnetite to respond to earth's magnetic field; we don't. Scientists recently found magnetite in human brain tissue, but don't know what it's doing there. It may be doing nothing and is merely a by-product of the way our tissues handle molecules of iron.

But we have words instead. We give 'directions'; we tell each other where to go.

The Aboriginal people in Australia migrated there from Asia around 30,000 years ago. Across this new land they followed songlines, which they believed were dreamed by a creator-spirit singing the plants, rocks, waterholes and land-marks into existence. There were song-paths across the sky, too. Songlines were verbal maps, threading the desert and the heavens with words.

Imagination and words are not a substitute for magnetite. Stories are a kind of mapping but are not navigation. Still, poems, songs, histories and geographies help us share with each other the way to go. We find stones that point north; we invent technologies; we have creativity and a sense of the past.

Compared to a storm petrel, however, returning to the same chink of Irish cliff from Africa year after year, it's easy to feel that's not enough. Our relationship with nature is ambivalent, and it's changing. We feel we have a right to control it, but we also like to use it as a mirror, something to think with about ourselves. Strong as an oak, free as a bird. But as the planet changes, the mirror is cracking. We can't use water and snow as images of purity now the seas are full of particles of our plastic, and layers of the carbon we loose into the air are embedded like tree rings under the North Pole.

———

The moon, too, is our ancient mirror. One way of looking at the moon is wish-fulfilment: it is the place to start again and do what we haven't been able to do on earth. The first recorded fantasy of a trip to the moon was written in the second century AD by the Syrian-Greek writer Lucian. Even then, this idea involved colonisation rights. Lucian described a boat navigating the Straits of Gibraltar suddenly lifted up by a waterspout. The voyagers land on the moon and get caught up in an interplanetary war: the kings of the moon and sun are fighting over colonising Venus.

Thirteen hundred years later, in *Orlando Furioso*, written by the Italian poet Ariosto between 1516 and 1532, an English knight flies to the moon on Elijah's chariot. Orlando has gone mad because the girl he loves has eloped with someone else. The English knight will bring back his wits, because on the moon you find everything you've lost on earth.

The German mathematician Johannes Kepler wanted a vivid way of demonstrating that you did not have to put earth at the centre of the universe. He published his first major work, *The Cosmographic Mystery*, in 1596, but even before, as a student, he'd begun a book on lunar astronomy, eventually published after he died as *The Dream*. It is an extraordinary piece of writing which includes an imaginary trip to the moon but also fleshes out in mathematical detail how space would look from the moon.

Wanting more – more resources than the planet has, a place where we can see from a different angle, find what we've lost on earth or get what we never had – is wanting the moon. If we've used up treasure here, let's move on to the next world. If we've fouled up this nest, fly to a new one. This lunar beauty . . . Finding in a new place what you've lost in the old is the dream of every migrant.

We destroy, but we also reclaim. The Mesopotamian marshes of southern Iraq were once the world's third largest wetland, a floodplain where the Euphrates and Tigris rivers divided into a network of tributaries meandering and pulsing south to the Arabian sea. For birds travelling from Central Africa to northern

Europe or Asia and back, these marshes were a vital stopover and refuelling site. Saddam Hussein drained them, turning the huge, once-teeming delta of reed beds into a dry, salt-encrusted desert. But now local people and Iraqi conservationists have restored the marshes. The reed beds are buzzing and twittering with life again. In Eden, at least, the harbingers are back.

Lodestone

I am Magnes the shepherd who found a pebble
stuck to a nail in his boot and discovered the mineral
Attract. I am Heinz Lowenstam, geologist from Silesia
who identified magnetite in tooth caps
of a homing mollusc. I am magnetotactic bacteria
knitted with crystals which orient to earth's
magnetic field. I am also your garden robin
who reads geomagnetic lines the way you scan
a newspaper, navigating folded thunderclouds at night
by neural pathways of Cluster N wired to my left eye
from light-processing regions of the brain.

I am the photoreceptor protein which draws young
monarch butterflies hatched on a month-long
journey to the same old Mexican forest their ancestors
            knew.
I am salamander, spiny lobster, bee, crocodile and whale
and also that flock of cranes passing silently over the
            moon.
I am fish, mammal, fungi and bird. I am two billion
            years
of life-forms steering by the minerals of which I am
            made
and molecular feel for the pull of the earth.
What about us, poor wanderers with no inner compass?
You inscribe the globe. You map, you have words,
you foresee your death. Isn't that enough?

Gun

Case-toughened breech inlaid with two pair
platinum lines. Steel tang lock
engraved with heads of hounds enclosed in foliage.
A scrolling serpent and a figured walnut stock.

Steel barrel, bolt escutcheons, chequered grip,
etched mount, back-action locks. Grip safety-catch
behind the trigger-guard. A cut-down butt,
steel ramrod-pipe plus brass-tipped ramrod.

Rainproof pan, shell finial, butt-cap. Rotation,
recoil. Look, a twin bore and extended magazine.
Piston. Stress, slide, hammer, pivot, bolt.
Noble. Rod. Device. Cartridge. The axial groove.

Assemble. Washer. Transverse tongue.
Cheek-gauge and shoulder-gauge. Thumb-hole,
hinge, flange and firing pin. Cylinder.
Double action, yes. Screw-bracket. Nut.

The annular chamber. The alarm call. Target
and observation post. The running of the deer.
A glazing eye. Scut and whisker. Trophy.
Tinder. Tender. Final. Finial. Disappeared.

End of the Line

I am standing at the end of the District Line
beyond Putney Bridge in the Old Store
of the Natural History Museum, a forest
of glass eyes, beside giraffe heads mounted on necks
like gingham lilies, each a different length.
The ears fan out for danger like gold leaves
from what had been a stereo of coclia and brain

checking for lion in the gullies.
The highest head, monsieur, is male
watching over his herd from the back
just where Myall's *Rules for Flower Arrangement
in the Drawing-Room* advise to slot the focal stem.
Behind him, a Hoolock gibbon's shrunken head
and brown eyes under his sad white tiara

and a wild ass of the Bible. Antelope brows
on mahogany shields, thousands of each species
inscribed with the place and the date
of a hunt. This is the underworld library of death
but you'd never guess. Anyone would take
this warehouse in a side road for a factory,
not the stilly realm where Persephone sits enthroned

and Nature ticks the extinction boxes one by one;
Hades arrived at by airlock and a puddle –
a slot for the hoist which levers giant auroch

or other large latecomers to their last bolt-hole –
whose greenwater sump-breath wells
into carefully calibrated air
like a rumour of greed in the human soul.

Sea Catch

What luck! A harbour
seal, *phoca vitalina,*
albino. Unique.

Whiskers lifted, look,
a face on him of gentle
curiosity.

Shot 1903.
The left eye socket empty
and the other eye

veiny crimson glass
like a rosy marble lost
in wet meadow grass.

The Mirror of Nature

Svalbard. Crack of a bubble, caught
ten thousand years in ice and now released.
Water has eaten the island's underhang.
At the glacier's core, carbon archives
have been identified, sooty bindweed
like the black line of Brünnich's guillemots –
the thick-billed murre, recorded as far off
as California – now zipping up
the quick gold of an Arctic horizon.

Eden, they say, as they always have.
All this is Creation, made for us to enjoy.
What can we do with a mind
that told itself jaw-cracking lies
then patted itself on the back? That knew
it was a bit of a bastard, but richer for the devil
in it; always so sure it was washable-clean
and could be redeemed by worldwater – so pure,
so green – and by *religio*, meaning 'a tie'?

But no tie endures. Milk-gothic spires
slide into the sea. Feather whips of zooplankton –
the dinoflagellates, eukaryotic protists
and foraminifera in the kingdom of protozoa
on whom we all depend – drift-ride to shore
on sparking waves plated, floe by floe,

with particles of plastic.
Tidewater glaciers unleaven
like loaves deliquescing back into dough.

Rabbit on the Moon

Fly to the moon as dusk comes on
and you'll see twelve celestial signs light up

like the *tapetum lucidum* of a stag
crossing the lane at night, looking at you

in the beam of your headlight.
Whose light is whose? There they are, twin

animal eyes into which you fling your dreams
when this world of men and all they ask

becomes too difficult. New light, here I come:
pour everything you are in here and start again

like the god who hurled a rabbit
at the inner segment of the moon.

See yourself up there, only visible when she's full.
Pure, beautiful, a door cut into time . . .

Remember the Spanish friar, shipped
to the New World, who spent seventy years

on Aztec grammar, Aztec lives,
Aztec myths, marriages and syntax

set down in Náhuatl, the dying language
of just one beloved tribe.

The Camden Telescope-Making Class

(In honour of Maggie Aderin-Pocock)

I'm leaving this sessile globe behind
to look for something better. A floating astronaut
steps from the glazed cover of a library book

and talks to me. Let me polish with satin cloths
my catadioptric reflector, home-grown
refraction and reflection which combine

in a field of view that's aberration-free.
I shall point it at the sky, and greet from afar
the *deus absconditus* himself. I plan to chart

the secret life of a mirror, chemical reactions
in each gas ring of Saturn, the objective dunes
of starlight a billion and a half years old,

the meteor's polychrome heart
in falling threads of albumen and gold
and every one of Jupiter's blue moons.

Letter to a Portuguese Cosmologist

'The Universe has no doors and no edges. There is
nothing stopping us from seeing what is going on in
any direction except the cosmological horizon.'
> – Pedro Ferreira, *The State of the Universe*

You talk of Gödel, Pedro, truths that can't be proved,
and the surface-of-last-scatter origins of light.
You pit tokens of dark matter, shrinking us, against
a mysterious safety pushing everything further apart,
but don't know how to answer where you're from.
You look for things that do not shine,

a mathematics of connectedness
in what the rest of us see
as spotted lacquer. Then add in Africa
where both your grandfathers were born. Shanty-
                                        towns,
streetcorner Kwaito music, glottal grammar
of too-quick-to-follow Xhosa chat shows,

acacia tines on sulphurous horizons
and surnames you recognise from Portugal
on fading turquoise petrol-station signs.
We don't know, you say, *how the first stars*
were born. If the universe wraps round itself
we should see tapestries of repeating lights,

distant copies of ourselves, our galaxy
and neighbours as they were in the past.
I'm at the kitchen table, night flaunting
her dark energy, and the moon above my head.
All that pushing apart! We close our prayers
on open numbers, *three*, *five*, *seven*, *nine*,

most inward when most looking out.
We come home to ourselves, following
a silver-paper trail among elliptic nebulae,
light-paths and strings of misalignment,
rough space that's never empty
and the hot dense core of stars.

Advertisement: The Lunar Registry

'This clear-view folder engraved with your own name
on a hundred per cent Cotton Ledger stock
with certificate borders elegantly lithographed
gives latitude, longitude and the Claims
Register number of your ownership. It contains
the sample deed for your acre of the Moon
and your membership in Lunar Republic,
official Website of the Moon. The future of the Moon
sitting up there in her mushroom lustre,
innocent as a newborn, is in your hands:
settlement, tourism development, industrial land.

Is that you listening to Frank Sinatra
on your birthday all alone? *Fly Me to the Moon!*
Virgin Galactic are planning a Space Hotel.
They land, or they will, with a heat-free
feathering system, kind on the environment
and safe safe safe. It's all arranged.
If you already own the hottest property on earth
the only better view is outer space.
What have you to lose? A million dollars
to the Moon and back, only five times
the chartered flight from Chennai to Dubai!

You also get mining rights. Prospecting for Helium 3,
the fusion-reactor fuel, rarer on earth than platinum,
must be high on every list of things to do

on the Moon. Space tourism's here to stay.
Only a fool would pass up the Sea of Tranquillity
with Tom Cruise and George Bush Senior
next plot along. Fancy a château by scenic Sea of Cold
on our roses-and-cream peninsula? How about
the Lunar Alps? There's so much to choose from.
Take my favourite, the Bay of Rainbows,
or the Edeny, dark-fruit-magnificent Lake of Dreams.'

Sharing Space

How far can you go? What does Fate
hold now by way of soothsaying?
The night before 9/11

a million Swainson's thrushes
must have flown
over the towers. Their road songs

have been recorded other years
on just that date
in the skies above Manhattan.

Farming the Wind

White cutlass on a space march to nowhere.
Knives hidden in cloud – slicing thorax,
breast-muscle, wings and liver
of osprey, plover, peregrine –
creating this spectral litter
of dead and dying biological masterpieces.

O birds who weave worlds together,
how nothing in your fossil footprint
prepared you for this. We are Odysseus' men
opening a skin bag expecting treasure
and getting blown to shipwreck
by all the winds of heaven.

If only the birds, said King Solomon, possessed
our rituals for detecting the presence of Belial
like burning a black cat's afterbirth
and sprinkling the ashes in your eye.
If only birds could see the wind atlas
we consult as we position our turbine.

The Marshes of Eden

(for Gwen at twenty-five)

We carry loss with us, as if we'd had a share
in when the world was new – some Garden
we don't know but must be the Home we left.

We dreamed of whispering wetgrass, the Everglades
beyond the freeway-turn for Disney World
where we saw through a glass-bottomed boat

one manatee afloat; quite possibly asleep.
You were eight, a small girl
laughing in a pedigree Keeshond T-shirt

and a tangle-cloud of wild-silk old-gold hair.
Heart like a wheel . . .The world turns
and I'm bartering in Bombay

for your birthday present,
the Goddess of Security,
and dreaming of Al-Qurna triangle

where the River Shatt al-Arab is born
and Tigris joins Euphrates, where Eden began
and backwaters melt from the mountains of Iran

to glimmer among reclaimed wetlands:
the ancient stopover
for sacred ibis, marbled teal.

Children of Storm

The new garden is an empty yard paved in pink and yellow stone. We've cut down leylandii taking all the light and there are no trees. I've seen a wren once, and two goldfinches. But it's July, birds will be finding food elsewhere. We'll have to wait till we plant trees, grass and bushes. My daughter has fitted her stuff into her tiny new room and left for work in Colombia, and there's a lot to do to turn this into a home. But we love it; these back gardens now seem normal.

But they're not normal – not in the age of migration with billions of people moving unhoused across the globe.

Thousands of migrations are smooth and happy, but this book is about the crossing, the journey. A million new immigrants enter the United States legally every year but thousands come in illegally, especially from and through Mexico. Cubans often arrive via Isla Mujeres, a small island off the Yucatan coast which they reach on home-made craft. In south Mexico, migrants from Guatemala, Honduras and El Salvador arrive in Tabasco and Chiapas. It is a dangerous border: corrupt police and immigration agents exploit them. Three Mexican National Migration Institute Officers were recently caught on video chasing a Honduran migrant with a machete into the Usumacinta River that borders Guatemala. They watched her struggle with the current until local villagers rescued her.

Mexico's northern border is even more dangerous. Barricading it, to keep illegal migrants and drug traffickers out of the United States, involves three operations called *Gatekeeper* in California, *Safeguard* in Arizona, and in Texas *Hold-the-Line*. The border is a patchwork of walls and cameras; supporters of the 'Border Fence Project' want a double fence along all 1,952 miles. Opponents say the fence destroys animal habitats and stops animals migrating or reaching water. They also say it doesn't work. Anyone with wire-cutters can get through the fence, and migrants also detour through the Sonoran Desert and Baboquivari Mountains.

The Mexican government has condemned the fence. So has the Governor of Texas (who wants better support for legal migration, instead) and the Mayor of Laredo, a town of 236,000 inhabitants on the river's north bank. 'These people are sustaining our economy by 40 per cent,' the Mayor says, 'and I'm gonna close the door on them and put up a wall? You don't *do* that!'

Thousands die trying to cross. Many drown in the Rio Grande, others die from heatstroke and dehydration in the desert, or in road accidents while chased by Border Patrol. As vulnerable as migrating birds, they are also shot by Border Patrol, vigilantes and the people-smugglers, there called 'coyotes'.

Casa del Migrante in Tijuana provides temporary lodging to people trying to cross. One worker there, describing in a podcast why they keep trying, says, 'Three months trying to cross and cross, even losing their lives, is better than go back. They borrowed money. They can't go back.'

This scenario is so familiar there is now an iPhone game about driving illegal migrants into the United States. In *Smuggle Truck* you dodge bullets from the drug mafia and border guards, tilt your pickup to catch babies bouncing out at the back as your cargo gives birth, and get them to the border where 'The Star-Spangled Banner' strikes up and you get a green card – and your score.

The Australian government uses a similar game to try and change attitudes to immigration. *Kick A Migrant* begins with immigrants huddled like lemmings on an Australian cliff: you see how far back into the sea you can kick them. But when your migrant splashes down, your inbox scolds you. 'That one came with a business degree! He's a Scout leader now, he gives jobs to Australians and owns a convenience store. Net loss to the economy of your kick – five hundred thousand a year.'

That sea drowns many real migrants. The detention centre on Christmas Island, 2,600 kilometres north-west of Perth, currently overflowing with people from Afghanistan and Sri Lanka, holds migrants while their claims for refugee status are assessed. In December 2010 the islanders watched helpless from a cliff as asylum-seekers – men, women and children in a boat from Indonesia – drowned or were battered to death on the rocks.

Since 2005 a European Agency based in Warsaw called Frontex has co-ordinated patrol boats and border guards controlling illegal immigration into the European Union. Many come west into Greece, from Afghanistan, Pakistan and Bangladesh, either by land from Turkey or in boats to the islands. Many others come from Africa. The independent, US-based Migration Policy Institute believes there are 8 million illegal African immigrants in the European Union. From West Africa they often go to the Cape Verde Islands, or the Canary Islands, where between twelve and thirty thousand arrive every year. They are too weak to walk or stand. When a boat approaches, the harbour fills with tents, hospital beds, police, sirens, wheelchairs and helicopters. Fishermen find bodies caught in nets. Lining the harbour, among the pleasure boats, are piles of bright-painted wooden fishing boats in which a hundred people have sat for many days. These are a health hazard and are cleaned, before being crushed, by men with protective clothing. Sometimes dead bodies are found in them.

Outside the Senegalese capital Daka is the poor suburb of Thiaroye. It was once a fishing village, but the villagers' traditional fishing can't compete with overfishing by huge European trawlers. This is the launch pad for thousands of young West Africans trying to reach the Canary Islands.

When the *passeurs* (traffickers) come through, hundreds of young men sign up, desperate to get to Europe. Women whose sons have already died in that attempt try to argue them out of it. Meanwhile, families from other rural areas club together to pay the *passeurs* to send their boys across the Sahara and out from Libya in little boats. In March 2009, 400 drowned in one night. They were packed into three small fishing boats and had come from Lagos, Accra, Addis Ababa, Nairobi, Yaounde, Banjul. From Egypt, Somalia, Ghana, Nigeria, Tunisia, Algeria, Morocco, Gambia and Cameroon but also from Bangladesh, Syria and Pakistan. They were hoping, said one of the few survivors, now in prison in Libya, for 'a better life'.

It has always been tough being a Mediterranean island. Through the centuries the islands have been invaded by Crusaders, Saracens, Venetians, the Templar Knights and the Ottomans, and now it is especially on islands that detention centres multiply. Like Aeneas sailing from North Africa to Sicily and then Italy, migrants leave Libya in these tiny frail boats (making them is an industry now) and go north. They land up in Crete, Sicily, Lampedusa or Sardinia and hope like Aeneas to reach Italy eventually. Or else they go to Spain.

Like long-winged birds who can only glide over sea, they try to find the shortest sea crossing. They often follow exactly the same south-north and east-west journeys as migrant birds (who also depend on the islands to stop over, rest and refuel). If you superimposed human and avian journeys on a world map, many lines would become one. Over the Strait of Gibraltar, over the Bosphorus or coming up from South America to North, human migrants face the same hostile planet as the birds: desert and sea, mountain and storm – and predators.

They are often blown off-course to Malta, needing medical help, screening, food and a place to sleep. They don't want to be there and the Maltese don't want them, but EU rules say asylum-seekers must make their claim in the first EU country they enter. Maltese ministers say their whole island is now a detention centre.

The EU agency Frontex helps the Maltese patrol their waters with helicopters and speedboats, but cannot turn back ships in international waters. If they see migrants turn up in distress they have to rescue them.

'We give them food, water, blankets, fuel, maps, things like that, and say, the best thing for you is to turn round and go back where you come from, because there is no future for you to enter that country,' said the Director of Frontex in 2007.

'Our fishermen feel overwhelmed,' says the commander of the Maltese maritime squadron. 'Their boats are built for six. Suddenly thirty migrants are trying to get in, too, and the boat turns over.'

***

A robin, once he's won his territory, fiercely defends it against other robins, often to the death. So do we. In every country, earlier immigrants resent new ones and try to keep them out. From the beginning of mass migrations to America in the 1880s, there were calls for restrictions and immigration laws. The Chinese Exclusion Act, Alien Contract Labor Law, Quota Laws, National Origins Act.

Twenty years ago, when my daughter was small, I lived in Greece. Albanian immigrants were then a new phenomenon. The same Albanians are now the naturalised fathers of children persecuting Pakistani and Somali immigrants – to keep Greece, they say, for the Greeks.

The Sangatte refugee camp opened in 1999 half a mile from the Channel Tunnel. It closed in 2002. Between 2004 and 2009 the number of illegal immigrants detected trying to enter Britain from France and Belgium trebled. Hundreds of Tunisians sleep rough today in the woods outside Paris. They have crossed desert and sea, realised their dream and want work. But there are 24 million Europeans out of work too. Now they want to go home.

In the UK a new Border Agency was created in 2008. Its parent agency is the Home Office and its job is 'to protect the UK border'. Many of its employees work at checkpoints at Calais, whose Chamber of Trade spends £12 million a year securing the port area, and blames Britain's immigration system for thousands of people on their land trying to climb into lorries and trains for the UK.

UK tabloids keep a tally of capture. Thirteen Afghans and two Iranians in a Hungarian-registered lorry of light bulbs, two Vietnamese in a load of nappies; four Afghans in a lorry of champagne; three Afghans, one Palestinian and an Iraqi in a shipment of bananas; ten people in a truck of sofas bound for Wrexham; eight in a truck of mozzarella cheese for Newmarket; twelve Afghans hiding in a thirty-two-foot Christmas tree; eighteen in a lorry of Spanish lettuces; a sixteen-year-old Vietnamese girl curled up with a white stuffed rabbit and surrounded by electrical wiring in sweltering conditions, squeezed behind the dashboard of a car. Three Afghans were found in a truck of Sainsbury's toilet rolls driving from the Czech Republic to Northfleet in Kent. 'Bidding', said the *Sun*, 'for a soft life in Britain.'

Recently a German truck driver drove off the ferry at Dover and heard singing in the back of his lorry. He drove to a police station and police arrested twelve men: four from Iran, four from Afghanistan, four from Iraq. Six were under sixteen. They had been singing to celebrate arriving in Britain.

<hr>

Asylum means 'the place which can't be plundered' and was a sacred concept in archaic Greece. At an altar, you were safe. You were a recognised suppliant, you had crossed into sacred space and anyone who violated your asylum was accursed. But the first reliably dated event in the history of Athens, a hundred or so years before democracy began, was the betrayal of asylum.

In 632 BC an Athenian nobleman named Cylon attempted a coup d'état at Athens. He captured the Acropolis, but was besieged there and sought asylum in the Temple of Athena. He escaped, but the rulers persuaded his less fortunate supporters to leave asylum and stand trial. They promised to spare their lives, but the suppliants were rightly wary and tied a rope to the goddess's statue as they came out in order to maintain contact with asylum. The rope broke, or was cut, the rulers claimed the goddess had repudiated her suppliants and the suppliants were stoned to death. But the rulers had violated the law against killing suppliants so their clan was cursed. This curse was still significant 200 years later in the democracy, and was used politically against their descendants. Asylum was a political issue before democracy began and has remained so ever since.

Today, supporters of an Open Borders policy in the UK call for the abolition of border controls, because they create worse suffering and human rights abuses; they believe the free movement of peoples should be recognised as a universal human right. But the UK is a small island, too.

In the last ten years a stamp saying LOC – for Lack of Credibility – has appeared on files as a reason to refuse asylum. One small mistake in any part of your statement is a reason to disbelieve all your testimony. Applicants are held in detention centres while a decision is made either to let them stay or to deport them to the country they came from.

The UK has thirteen detention centres, formally rebranded in 2002 as Immigration Removal Centres. Some of these are run by private companies contracted by the Government. They are for people seeking asylum, or people thought to be illegal immigrants. Asylum-seekers are put in them when they arrive and held while they wait for their case to be decided, or wait to be deported if it is refused. The conditions of these centres have been criticised by the UK Inspector of Prisons. A report by the Medical Foundation for the Care of Victims of Torture and Medical Justice speaks of 'systematic abuse' within them; of hunger strikes, riots, suicides; complaints of rape, assault, intimidation and lack of information about basic rights.

People will do anything to keep out of them. In 2004 twenty-three Chinese migrant workers died in the mudflats of Morecambe Bay. Nick Broomfield's film *Ghosts* (2006) recreated their story. Having paid snakehead gangs to smuggle them on a year-long journey across Asia and Europe, they were put to work by gang-masters. The *Aeneid* ends with indigenous Italians making war on the Trojan refugees, and the Chinese immigrants were beaten up by British rivals who took their cockle-sacks. So they picked cockles at night, stuck in the mud as the tide came in, and drowned.

⌇⌇⌇⌇⌇⌇

Migration is a lottery. Thousands of migrating animals and people die. Conditions in the new place are often very hard. For humans there are further psychological costs. A friend of mine, a psychiatrist for the homeless, was called out recently in the night because one of his patients, a Muonyjang from South Sudan, suddenly had to be hospitalised.

Several years after coming to Britain this man and his mother were reunited with his elder brother. All three escaped massacre in South Sudan when the boys were eight and five. To give the family more chance of surviving they decided to split up. The elder was recruited as a child soldier. He saw and did unspeakable things but eventually escaped, was rescued in Ethiopia by the UN, and is now a successful businessman.

The mother went with the younger son to Egypt; they reached Britain, he grew up and went to a British university, but suddenly broke down and ended up homeless on the London streets.

Migration may bring new life. But the loss of home and the traumas you endure, the reason you have to flee in the first place, may take its toll long afterwards.

⌇⌇⌇⌇⌇⌇

Turn the crystal of 'migration' and you get 'home'. In Britain it is the Home Office which deals with immigration and detention – and also with deportation. In the 1990s, the Home Office began what medical agencies call outsourcing abuse, hiring private companies – called escort agencies or security solutions firms – to accompany refused asylum-seekers back to their countries of origin by force.

This is a new industry. Reports on it by charities have found multiple abuses. Escorts are on hourly pay, have a financial incentive (no bonus unless they return their deportee to his country of origin), a record of criminal assault is no bar to employment and their actions are not open to public scrutiny.

In 2010 at Heathrow three escorts from the security solutions firm G4S boarded a plane for Luanda with an Angolan man, Jimmy Mubenga. Passengers heard Mubenga shouting that he didn't want to leave his wife and children, that he couldn't breathe. His last words were, 'They're trying to kill me.' The aircraft returned to the terminal; Jimmy Mubenga was pronounced dead in hospital. Escorts are allowed to use control techniques approved by the Prison Service but pushing a deportee's head between his legs is forbidden. Death from it is called positional asphyxia.

These three escorts are currently suspended and under investigation for manslaughter. One recently posted a photo on his Facebook page showing two south Asian men sitting on an aeroplane, one of whom has his seatbelt across his shoulder as in a car. Comments of this escort's Facebook friends laugh at the seatbelt mistake, mock the men as 'depos' and say they should be in handcuffs shouting 'kill me now'.

This new legal industry of 'security solutions' and escort agencies mirrors the illegal one of people-smuggling. Two lots of money made out of people who have none. Trapped between criminals and governments like wildebeest between crocodiles and lions, migrants are big business, except to themselves.

Migration is essential to life on earth. Cells dismantle their structure and start again, or migrate to form new embryos. Life-forms migrate constantly, our species is *homo viator*, our civilization began with migration. 'Asylum-seekers' implies a 'they' who want something from 'us' and ignores what immigrants give. As the Mayor of Laredo says, migrations sustain society. But because of our expanding population, and what we are doing to the earth, migration is at unprecedented levels. People emigrate from desperate need. Like blackpoll warblers in hurricanes, they suffer terrible losses. Reaching countries in recession with rising unemployment, many find no work, merely hostility. British readers of a 2009 newspaper article on Gambian families of migrants drowned in boats off Libya commented online, 'The UK's not a dumping ground for illegal immigrants!' 'They're like burglars breaking into your home demanding food.' 'If they want a better life they should stay in their country and improve matters there.' The religious requirement behind Western religions is sympathy. *Help the poor as you would a stranger, for you were a stranger too.* What hope is there, in a world where nations are closing the portcullis?

Mara in Latin means 'bitter'. In North European folklore, Mara is a nightmare demon of horror and death. Buddhist Mara is a demon of illusion: once the Vedic demon of drought, he now spreads terror through deception, threatening us by obscuring truth. He tempted the Buddha too, who touched the earth and realized enlightenment so that Mara disappeared. The Proto-Indo-European root *mer*, 'to die', and Sanskrit *mara*, 'obstacle, death', stand behind these Maras, but by phonetic accident they resemble the Masai name for the river at the end of the wildebeest's journey. Since I witnessed what happens at that river, 'Mara' has come to me to represent bitter losses, struggle, barriers and obstacles, but also the triumph of survival. Like the wildebeest, migrants cross over to create new cultural life.

Hope, that word which powers migration, lies in staying open to what is happening. In not looking away, questioning those who operate the portcullis, exposing and resisting cruelty in implementing government policies, paying attention to the developed world's responsibility for displacements (fished-out seas, corporate over-use of resources which uproots people and destroys their land), keeping sympathy with other people's stories, seeing their experience as part of our own. Some readers of that newspaper did reply to those comments. 'It is only by the Grace of God,' said one, 'that you are not one of these unfortunates. You are an accident of birth, as they are.' Hope springs from that faculty which other animals don't seem to need but *homo viator* needs more than ever today. Compassion – and beyond that, empathy.

The Desert and the Sea

'I might not survive. I knew this. The only way
is risk your life. In Eritrea you're never free;
if I want to go to another city I must pay.
In Europe I go anywhere I like.

My first time, I was with a hundred families.
Big boats came after us. After five days at sea
we were back in Libya, in prison. Children
and pregnant women, all in prison.

I tried again. Out of one hundred, twenty-five
may get to Italy. You will not know. Some die
in the sea, some end in prison and some die
in the desert where you don't die quick.

Is it worth the risk? I cannot say yes
or no. It depends how your soul
buckles under the burden
of months – no, years – of *almost*.'

Ghost Ship

You have to get out. But this is how you imagine
you might go, when you wake at night afraid
of moving on, from Gambia or Guinea Bissau,

and hear the redslick in your temple beat
like waves around the ghost ship
discovered off Ragged Point, Barbados.

A six-foot yacht, adrift. No name, no flag
and a phantom crew, eleven young men
in green, red, orange, blue,

mummified in salt of their own sweat.
You can't shake out of your head
that airline ticket from Senegal, the note

in a dead boy's pocket – *Excuse me, this is the end,
sorry to my family in Bassada* – saying how the skipper
disappeared before they left Cape Verde;

how he could have jumped, like his friend,
when they were towed. And how one night
the rope was slashed by a machete.

Orestiada

(for Kerin Hope)

Any weakening in Fortress Europe
will show in ripples of the icy Hebros
still carrying a memory
of the floating head of Orpheus.
Twenty years ago, the novelty
was Immigrant Market at Theseion:

Albanians, squatting on unravelled
plastic tartan, offering cut-price replicas
of everything under the sun.
You invested, Kerin, in a present
for your god-daughter: a cochineal
post-Soviet My Little Pony.

In Athens today, you see *No Mosques*
and *This is Greece* sprayed over the square
as Albanian vigilantes chase the Afghans out.
People-traffickers from Troy
throw their customers in the Hebros
and asphyxiate stowaways in trucks

but they keep coming, over a forest frontier
of landmines and razor wire,
carrying toddlers and plastic bags

to hide behind a furniture factory
in suburbs of Orestiada, the city named
for the boy who knifed his mother and went mad.

Wetbacks

(for Issam Kourbaj)

'Mexicans cross a river, Cubans cross a fucking ocean!!
Cubans are the wetbacks, not Mexicans.'
           – Blogger at Urban Dictionary.com

We're sitting on paint-splashed stools in your studio
sipping wine. You talk of Damascus, show me your
                                  design
for postboxes floating in air. 'How about those
                           chairs, Issam?'
'Ah Cuba! Ruth, the beach was dark with them.

A sea of broken chairs! They lash them together
and push off. After seeing that, I found chairs
in skips, and throw-outs from the restaurant downstairs,
to make a Migrant Monument in their honour.'

You pile up legs of beech and deal. When the chips
are down, this is all we need: a stack
of splintered wood. Like José Luis, fridge
repair-man from Havana, who took five days

to make it to Isla Mujeres Mexico
spread-eagled on inner tubes
bound to a chair-back powered by
a *put-put* used for irrigating fields.

Maltese Fishing Boat and Broken Net

They set off in a Phoenician fishing smack
with the Eye of Horus kohl-outlined –
the pupil turned in as if squinting –
on a double-ended hull.

High bows of ochre, red and green
swoop waves now indigo,
now khaki, transverse and longitudinal,
which will mean a bit of a swell.
She's built to take six men, with nets
for amber jack, stone bass, white bream.

Here's a *cayuco* – the kind one sees limping in
to Tenerife, where migrants are trucked
to La Esperanza Detention Centre
while the boat is sterilised and crushed –

so low in the water a hundred pairs of hands,
up to the elbows, are batting the waves.
Where's Frontex Patrol? She's broadside –
now she's turtle. They're clinging on, slipping,
pushing. Most can't swim. But some
splash over, grab the net, pull us down . . .

Cut the rope! What would *you* do?
We lose our catch but we get home.

A hundred are drowning –
why should we six die too?

The Place without a Door

Listen. There are dragons under cities,
monsters in white spaces on sea maps.
Sangatte is a commune on the coast of France
facing water which the English call English Channel,
a border for which many men, and women too,
have died. The name means Gap-in-Sand.
When we were there, we knew
it was The Place Without a Door.
Mark the spot in my brother's heart
where he built a cardboard shrine
for our wasteland jungle. Check the wall
where someone graffed, *Nous voulons de l'air*
pour nos enfants. The cement octagons
where we hid at night to rush the axle
of Spanish lorries. The bridge where my brother
jumped that train into the tunnel.

Immigration Counter and the Gates of Ivory

They're flying back to Canada, after summer in
                                              Mumbai.
'Think they're still awake now, Grandpa and Granny?'
Wails fill the cabin as lights go down
and we're in the Moonlight World of the Small
                                              Mammal
House at the Zoo. Her face is a fire-lit mask
as she settles their blankets and the rest of us try
looking this night in its indigo eye, pleated
like inner petals of a gentian. We doze
while in the Mumbai suburb where, let's suppose,
she grew up, her parents still flick through the photos.
Home was festivals, the kitchen, the shrine of a front
                                              room.
But that's over now, with the grandchildren abroad.

Light glimmers through the thicket of the aisle.
Roll on seven hours, we're in Passport Control
with a flight from Abuja. The family in transit from
                                              Mumbai
have papers fresh as snow
but here's an old guy from Nigeria, alone
with a string bag. Behind the officer in blue,
turning every page of my passport,
a kiosk of Travelex World Wide Money glows
like Santa's Magic Cave.

Then I'm through,
the Mumbai lot too. But for the old man
she's called a colleague. They winnow

his papers like a rice harvest. No Travelex for him.
A man may dream his wife returns, or he returns
to her, but dreams are shadow-customers. They flit
from the underworld through two doors – one horn,
one ivory. If your dreams pick
ivory, the ancestors are amusing themselves
I'm afraid, floating illusion upward to the living.
Dreams that arrive through horn come true
but how do you know? At the Styx
of the UK Border, a gentian blossom
is forcibly removed. We progress to Luggage Claim.
Indigo petals fade, curl and close on nothing.

The Apple Orchard in Ghosts

That moment in the film
when there's no more work in the fields

and the leather-collared bull-man
gangmaster shifts them to an orchard

harvesting its last fruit
before the Worcester Pearmains

and Red Falstaffs are torn up for ever.
Suddenly it's the 'People Will Say We're in Love' scene,

all trees, wicker baskets and sunlight,
from *Oklahoma*

and England is no longer grey mud
beyond the greasy windows of the minibus

but green – yes, and real people,
gentle and sad themselves,

in a misty kitchen
offering what passes for tea.

The Prayer Labyrinth

She went looking for her daughter. How many
visit Hades and live? Your only hope
is the long labyrinth of Visa Application
interviews with a volunteer from a charity
but you're not allowed to meet her.
You've been caught: by a knock on the door
at dawn, or hiding in a truck of toilet tissue
or just getting stuck in a turnstile.

You're on Dead Island: a Detention Centre.
The Russian refugees who leaped from the fifteenth
                                                    floor
of a Glasgow tower block to the Red Road
Springburn – Serge, Tatiana and their son
who, when immigration officers
were at the door, tied themselves together
before they jumped – knew what was coming.

Anyway you're here. Evidence of cigarette
burns all over your body has been dismissed
by the latest technology. You're dragged
from your room, denied medication
or a voice. You can't see your children,
they're behind bars somewhere else.
You go on hunger strike. You're locked
in a corridor for three days without water

then handcuffed through the biopsy
on your right breast. You've no choice
but to pray; and to walk the never-ending path
of meditation on *not yet*. Your nightmare
was home-grown: you're seeking sanctuary.
They say you don't belong. They give you
a broken finger, a punctured lung.

Purple Ink

She has waited three years for this. Too ashamed
to even half-tell the young woman in spectacles
tapping a purple biro on a desk

exactly what the soldiers did to her, each versatile
in his turn, she gets wrong *Date your mother was born*
and sees a stamp the colour of desert night descend on
her file.

Carpet Karaoke

New life forms are entering the world:
government agencies, like young dragons
on a moonlit beach, in a transitional period
of operation. Let's imagine you're standing
at Gatwick Airport in the Year of Our Lord
2008 and a Secretary is launching the UK
Border Agency to be a shadow to the Home Office.

Now let's suppose you slip out of the House
of Lords onto Cornish granite, and hammer
on the Great West Door of Westminster Abbey,
yearning to sing the Office of Compline.
Rays stream in through Gothic stone, lighting up
the eleven-circuit labyrinth embedded in the floor,
and the filigree rosette at its heart
signifying compassion and enlightenment

while shadows multiply under home floorboards
and Securicor blends with G4S
whose motto is *Securing Your World* –
yes, the escort agency, silent as the Chinese word
for secrecy, where a criminal record for assault
is no barrier as security escort; providing solutions
to the problem of not enough world to go round

in the shape of escorts trained in pain compliance
who have taken a shine to one particular technique
and compare notes on it on Facebook. Ride the 24
to the end of the line, studying case histories
from the Medical Justice Network, and you find
the word 'breathing' twined through them all
like flowers through a kelim.
They hand-and-leg-cuff their deportee,

double him up on the seat, three or four
to one, and push his head between his legs.
Think iron grinding ice, think don't-want-to-look.
'They fist-squeezed his testicles, kicked in
his ribs and his stomach.' He cried, they say,
they always say, for help. But fighting for breath
he can only shout at the floor.

Dancers with Bruised Knees

*(for Mark Baldwin, Siobhan Davies and the
dancers of the Rambert Dance Company)*

A rainy day in Chiswick. They are working on
The Art of Touch, dropping out now and then
to rewind bandages on ankles, stick a plaster
on a toe, do leg-warms at the barre.

Mark, born in Fiji, has invited me to watch
rehearsal. They're all from somewhere else.
'It's hard for them to come. It takes four
months to get a visa and never certain.
You're not allowed to bring dancers from abroad.'

Bodies hurtle over space, their calloused feet
accurate to music of glass and steel
by Domenico Scarlatti. Pieter, Gemma, Eryck,
Dane; Estela from Spain; Miguel

from Cuba – following Acosta, star
of *No Way Home*. They're here, they've made it.
Kirill from Latvia, Vanessa from Singapore.
Show foreigners hospitality, says the Bible,
for many have entertained an angel unaware.

They're wiping sweat, checking feet for scars
and strain. *Diagonal – long hop – ker dum! –*

and kneel. Stefano from Italy. 'Loosen your arms!'
Home is a white bird over the chasm.

Help the poor, say the verses. *Treat them fair*
just as you would a stranger, for you were a stranger
                                                            too.
'No matter where you're from,' the dancers say,
'you need the choreography. You have to know
exactly where you're going on the floor.'

I sit in the corner on a plastic chair.
Their steps, repeated over and over – the same
but different in each body – are a meeting-ground, a
                                                            prayer.
When they touch the floor

or touch each other, how do they pitch their body
and not get in their partner's way?
I was a foreigner and you welcomed me.
I see the world, the air, hang like a curtain
and swing apart for a single swan.

Where your feet are is all the home there is.
We dab the stage for certainty, we strangers
on the earth, the way an Indian dancer
touches the ground with her hand before coming on.

The Wanderings of Psyche

We migrate not only on the road but in the mind – and, we like to think, in the psyche. Escape literature, armchair travel and fantasy express our migrant souls. It's an attractive notion. Yeats's phrase 'pilgrim soul' was even taken as the title of an episode in the Eighties revival of the American TV suspense and science fiction series *The Twilight Zone*.

We also want to migrate after death. Migration is the great let's-get-out-of-here hope for our body, and we have always dreamed of our souls carrying it off too. Egyptians gave the dying soul equipment for the journey; many more modern religions treat dying as 'migration' to another body, another life or land. A better land, glimmering beyond this one like sky behind branches of a tree.

Hinduism says souls migrate from one life to another and each life is a pause in the cycle. After every life you are born again. *Shakuntala*, a Sanskrit play from the first millennium BC, tells the story of a king who has been cursed to forget his beloved. One day he hears a woman singing outside his window and feels a strange pang, as if reminded of something he loved in another life. The song, he says, seems 'to cling like a fragrance to my migrant soul'.

The Orphics believed the soul was on a perpetual journey to new reincarnations. Gold leaves found in Greek graves of the fourth-century BC were inscribed with instructions for the dying soul. Plato ended the *Republic* with a man who came back to life and said he had seen souls choosing their next life, then flying away like stars to be born again. 'Beautiful is the struggle,' says the dying Socrates at the end of Plato's *Phaedo*, referring to his belief in the transmigration of the soul, 'and the hope is great.'

'The Aspiration', a penitential poem by the seventeenth-century poet John Norris, speaks of getting out of the body up to heaven, and early Christianity took the myth of Psyche and Eros (or Cupid) as an allegory for the soul's search for God.

This story migrated into European folktale, but was written up first in Latin by a migrant of the second century AD in the satirical novel *The Golden Ass*.

Apuleius may have been a Berber. He was born in a Roman colony in what is now Algeria and went to Athens to study, then travelled to Italy, Asia Minor and Egypt. In *The Golden Ass* he tells the story of Cupid and Psyche. Cupid forbade Psyche, he says, to see his face. He visited her only at night and Psyche's sisters said that he must be a monster – she should check. So Psyche did and realised that her lover was the god of Desire. But her oil lamp dripped on his shoulder and Cupid woke, caught her looking and flew away. Psyche set off to find him and her hazardous journey culminated in a trip to the

Underworld to fetch a box of beauty for Cupid's mother, Venus. Opening this to take a little for herself, Psyche was over-powered by sleep. Cupid came to help and repacked the sleep in its box; then Jupiter made Psyche immortal and the pair, reunited, now live among the gods.

Christianity saw this story as an allegory of the soul in its search for divine love, which like Psyche we lose through our own fault. God forgives us as Cupid forgave Psyche. United with God, we find our divine home. Our *psyche* migrates to heaven.

———

While physical displacement is the main push factor in migration, psychological displacement is the motive force in imagination and creativity. Plato assumed a parallel between body, soul and society, or the body politic: they are metaphors for each other. In the *Republic*, damage and healing in one is an image for damage and healing in the others.

Freud described the ego as a 'frontier-creature' which polices the borderlands of identity and mediates between the world and the unconscious. The personality, he suggested, is formed partly by psychological 'displacement'. As we grow, and respond to what happens around us, we deal with painful feelings like anxiety, grief or anger by constructing defences against them. Displacement, that word which echoes also through explanations of migration, is one such psychological defence. We 'displace' our disturbing feelings into areas where they feel less threatening. By withdrawing from a trauma, the mind reroutes feelings about it on to something else and so transforms these feelings.

We go on doing this throughout our lives: we all displace unpleasant emotions into areas where they don't feel so destructive and may even be creative. But psychologists say that painters, theoretical scientists, philosophers, poets and mystics make particular use of withdrawal and displacement.

If you displace pain you escape it, not by denying it or distorting reality but by migrating to a different (and with any luck creative) perspective. You're not misunderstanding or denying the world, you know the massacre has happened, but you're making something of it. Goya paints *The Disasters of War*.

———

Seamus Heaney's phrase 'inner émigré' reminds us that artists have always had complicated relationships to exile, both outer and inner. The fifteenth-century Aztec prince Nezahualcoyotl became an inner émigré as a teenager, when a rival kingdom conquered his city of Texcoco. He fled into exile twice, but eventually got his city back. He brought it law, art, scholarship and aqueducts, made it the pre-Hispanic Athens of the Western World and went down in history as a warrior, architect and philosopher-king – but most of all as a poet, whose psyche was formed in exile.

Matisse was an inner émigré in a different sense. According to his biographer, a tension between the making of astonishing visible beauty and crippling anxiety (which is well-documented but was often invisible) marked his life as well as his work. Matisse 'the anxious, the madly anxious', a friend described him. His biographer conjures up a life marked by desperation, self-doubt, and a pain which required art to be a force of calm.

He said art should be about art, not life; a refuge from reality, 'devoid of troubling or depressing subject matter, like an armchair which provides relaxation from fatigue.'

But Matisse was not denying the reality around him. At forty-five he volunteered for service in the First World War, though was rejected because of his age. He was seventy when the Nazis entered France and although he had a visa for Brazil he refused to leave. 'I would have felt like a deserter,' he wrote to his son. Both his wife, from whom he divorced painfully in 1939, and his daughter Marguerite were active in the Resistance. Afterwards he was very shocked to hear that Marguerite had been imprisoned and tortured (she escaped from a cattle car that stalled on its way to a prison camp). But during the war, he withdrew to Villa Le Rêve, a house on the Côte d'Azur. He was diagnosed with cancer in 1941 and had to have surgery. He became isolated, shielding his art fiercely from politics. Long before, he had watched Renoir, very near death, painting with a brush strapped to his bandaged hand. 'I have never seen a man so happy,' said Matisse, 'and I promised myself then that when my time came, I would not be a coward either.'

Materials were hard to get in the war and Matisse turned to a new technique: the paper cut-outs which he called 'painting with scissors'. Afterwards, in 1947, he published *Jazz*, an artist's book of these cut-outs. Later, near death himself, he fastened bits of charcoal to a fishing-pole and drew faces of his grandchildren, whom he adored, on the blank ceiling above his bed.

We displace pain by transforming its presence in our lives into pattern. 'After great pain,' says Emily Dickinson, 'a formal feeling comes'. But such displacement also happens in the middle of trauma. Picasso, Matisse's friend and rival, painted *Guernica* in 1937 immediately after hearing that the most ancient centre of the Basque Country had been bombed in the Spanish Civil War. And it was in the 1560s, at the start of the Eighty Years War, that Bruegel painted *The Massacre of the Innocents* and *The Triumph of Death*.

———

The British space scientist Maggie Aderin-Pocock became a different sort of inner émigré. She was a second-generation immigrant: her parents came from Nigeria and her father saw Britain as his homeland. But the move and the marriage did not work, the parents separated and the little girl went to thirteen different schools. From the age of three, she turned to the moon. 'Outer space saw me through,' she has explained. She watched *Star Trek*. She fell in love with an astronaut on the cover of a library book. She was diagnosed with dyslexia, and her teachers said she must take up nursing, but at fifteen she saved to buy a telescope from Argos. It didn't work, so she made her own; she went on to study science, maths and astronomy at Imperial College.

Wonderful determination, but also powerful displacement. Hope, curiosity and intensity projected outwards – not in a flight to unreality or to fantasy, which would have denied the real pain of her life, but to the hard work and patterning of science, maths and astronomy, where hurt was irrelevant.

———

W. H. Auden's elegy for Freud portrays him as wanting us to be 'enthusiastic over the night' – the unconscious, presumably

– because of 'the sense of wonder it alone has to offer'. Around Freud, the poem sees 'fauna of the night': unconscious feelings, 'dumb creatures' who are also 'exiles', longing for 'the future that lives in our power'. It is a hopeful vision, of the unconscious as the source of imagination and transformation. The power to move our lives, the poem suggests (or suggests that Freud suggested), lies inside us invisible, dumb and estranged. If we encourage it we shift our alienated feelings into the light; we give them a new life, a 'future'.

This is the dream of every artist as well as every migrant. Tennyson said that ever since he was young he had thrilled to the phrase 'far far away'. This phrase and feeling are encapsulated in the song 'Over the Rainbow', sung by Judy Garland in *The Wizard of Oz* (1939) before the screen explodes into colour. The melody begins with an octave leap. Its first two notes ('some-where') are a musical migration like an uprooting of the self. Salman Rushdie calls it an anthem for all migrants; for anyone searching for where 'the dreams you dare to dream come true'.

At the film's end, the ruby slippers carry Dorothy home while she murmurs 'there's no place like home'. But then she discovers that the people at home were also her friends in Oz. 'So Oz finally became home,' says Rushdie. 'The imagined world became the actual world.' There is indeed, the film suggests, a place 'like' home. It is the place we create in our imagination.

Fantasy is not the same as imagination. Fantasy escapes reality by denying it. Imagination transforms it, lifting us from our current life to a colour-filled place which doesn't exist but might if we can make it. And so, like Psyche, we end up with a new life. Or, like Dorothy, we get our old home back but see it with new eyes.

The poet Jalāl ad-Dīn Muhammad Balkhī, or Rumi, was born in Balkh, one of the oldest cities in the world. The Arabs called it Umm Al-Belaad, Mother of Cities; the Greeks called it Bactra. It is now in northern Afghanistan. Rumi was born there in 1207, but his family left when he was a boy, in the face of Mongol invasions. They migrated to Konya, which is now in Turkey and was then the capital of the Sultanate of Rum. Rumi, often called Maulana, the Learned One, became the leading religious scholar in Konya's dervish community.

Dar is Persian for 'door'. Just as an open door is at the heart of the Christian icon of the Transformation, so a *dervish* transforms by opening doors. What opened the door for Rumi's poems was his friendship and mystic conversation with Shams of Tabriz, a wandering dervish. Then Shams disappeared, probably because Rumi's students became jealous. Shams was found in Damascus and brought back, but one December night he was called to the back door and vanished forever. He was probably murdered. In his grief, Rumi began writing poems. The spring of his poetry was loss and the mystery of recovery. As the bonds in the DNA molecule are broken so that the proteins can replicate the genetic code, and as cells migrate in the body to heal or to generate an embryo, so in the mind the drive to re-find and re-place what has been lost is the driving force behind both creativity and migration.

A shabby Georgian house in Spitalfields, in London's East End, is a monument to the imagination and hope behind migration.

Nineteen Princelet Street is an unrestored house built in 1719 for Huguenot silkweavers escaping Catholic persecution in France. In the nineteenth century it was inhabited by Irish immigrants escaping famine, and then by Jews escaping pogroms in Eastern Europe. In 1869, the Jews made a synagogue there. New immigrants from Poland formed in it a United Friends Friendly Society to help incoming immigrants. In the twentieth century, Bengalis lived in the area around it, and later on Somalis. It is now Britain's first Museum of Immigration. Artists working with immigrant children from local schools have created in it a permanent exhibition, *Suitcases and Sanctuary*. As on Ellis Island, this commemorates successive waves of immigrants, but does so through the eyes of the East End's current children.

This modest place embodies Britain over the centuries as a place of sanctuary and new life. It tells the story of a house, a parish and a city whose walls, as we know, were built by immigrants. Very quietly, it shows how multicultural Britain – and every modern, multilayered society – was made, just as the world was made, by migration.

The Wood Where Birds Die
for Christ and Rise Again

William Wey, sir, from Devon, on pilgrimage
to Jerusalem, between two worlds like a wind
off the desert. Make sure you carry candles,
cooking tools, a lantern – and a chamber pot
in case you are too sick to go on deck.

A chandler in Venice, by St Marks, will sell you
a feather bed for three ducats and buy it back
for one and a half, if you return. Look where I retrace
my steps, on this map whose green itineraries curl
like knotweed. A pack-path pinpoints recurrent miracles

like that Saracen story of songbirds in a certain wood
who die every Passion Sunday and come back to life
on Easter Day. Here is the river which bubbles
at Epiphany, between the singing of one vesper
and the next; and here you pass into a twilight zone,

the Palace of Loss where Hope began. The world
is not what you see. This is the seat of the soul
where inner and outer meet. You reach gold
pomegranates hanging in the mist; moon-milk
in a mountain cave; wild thyme; a scallop shell.

Only Here on Earth

'Earth is the region of the fleeting moment.
Will I have to go, like the flowers that perish?
Will nothing remain, not even my songs?
Is it only here on earth we come to know
our faces?' So wrote the teenage prince

exiled to Huexotzinco. Boughs of the pecan
tree, flash of a flycatcher's wing,
indigo wool in grey spice of a Tepanec rug.
Smoke rises over Mount Atloyan like foxing
on a mirror. Distant melodies – clay flute

and ocarina; and that tricksy pass
from cello to viola in the first-time bar
of the minuet. There's no other world.
Feather gloves lie in a patch of sun
on parquet floor. The perfect moment

comes to us in its own time:
planting bulbs for spring, hearing the purr
of a stranger's orange press
or laying the table, hunting four-
tined forks in the chaos of a cutlery drawer.

Matisse Writes a Postcard after the War

He's old. He's ill. He takes black ink
and watercolour to the patio
to sketch the only wine glass on his table.

The coiled thick stem; the little row
of blobs below the bowl –
a seed-pearl choker for a very slender throat –

and a candy smudge of thinning pink
within. This need to know the worst
but hope to hold . . . Beside the pale-rose tint

of water drying in grey circlets
and the eyelash line where he sketched
the hollow bulb, he writes *6th May*

1947. This is the glass in which I drink
the fresh and perfumed wine of Alsace.
À ta santé. Tous les jours que tu n'es pas là.

Prayer on an Orphic Gold Leaf

Don't be afraid. On your way you'll pass the rivers
Mnemosyne and Lethe. Don't drink the water –
you don't need any longer to remember or forget.
You're a lily closing on its stamen, the zendrum
of a heart in tremolo. You may hear music. Whip-rays
of light converge by the bed on a Book of Psalms
left by your last visitor. You are glass, annealing
to that celestial temperature where molecules
rearrange all inner stress to perfect surface tension
in a new, fused, tough material. In the distance
you'll see one pine-tree, needle-leaves
clumped in three balls on a trunk like black bone
twisted in wind. You'll know
you are making, and coming, home.

Open Door: after Rumi

(for Nikos Stavroulakis)

What is not exile? Beginning is flight.
(The end is free flow of breath.)

I am inside your looking, I wait to be light.
(Rustle of water, of wind.) Cling
to the surface. Hold to the depths
as tired eyes look forward to sleep.

Why should I seek? (Rusty cliffs glow
in the lake. Tremble of aquamarine.
White mosque silhouette on the peak.)
A hand closes and opens like wings.

You are where I am. Let go
what you thought you had lost.
Praise those who wake early in grief.

Time to Fly

You go because you heard a cuckoo call. You go
                                              because
you've met someone, you made a vow, there are no
                                              more
grasshoppers. You go because the cold is coming, spring
is coming, soldiers are coming. Plague, flood, an ice age,
a new religion, a new idea. You go because the world
                                              rotates,
because the world is changing and you've lost the key.
You go because you have the kingdom of heaven in
                                              your heart
and the kingdom of hell has taken over someone else's
                                              heart.

You go because you have magnetite in your brain,
                                              thorax, tips
of your teeth. Because the grass is green
over the hill and there's gold, or more likely bauxite,
inside the hill. You go because your mother is dying
and only you can bring her the apples of the Hesperides.
You go because you need work.

You go because the astrologers say so – the sea
is calling – your best friend bought a motorbike
in America last year. You go because the streets are paved
with gold and besides, your father went when he was
                                              your age.

You go because you have seventeen children and the
                              Lord will provide,
because your sixteen brothers have parcelled up the land
and there's none left for you. You go because the waters
                              are rising,
an ice sheet is melting, the rivers are dry,

there are no more fish in the sea. You go because God
has given you a sign – you had a dream – the potatoes
                              are blighted
because it is too hot, too cold, you are on a quest for
                              knowledge
and knowledge is always beyond. You go because it's
                              destiny,
because Pharoah won't let you light candles on Friday at
                              sundown.
Because you are looking for

an enchanted lake, the meaning of life, a tall tree to nest in.
You go because travel is holy, because your body
is wired to go, you'd have a quite different body and
                              different brain
if you were the sort of bird that stayed. You go
because you can't pay the rent, creditors lie in wait for
                              your children
after school. You go because Pharoah has hogged
the oil, electricity and paraffin so all you have on your
                              table
are candles, when you can get them.

You go because there's nothing left to hope for;
because there's everything to hope for and all life is risk.

You go because someone put the evil eye on you
and barometric pressure is dropping. You go because
                                                you can't cope
with your gift – other people can't cope with your gift –
you have no gift and the barbarians are after you.

You go because the barbarians are gone, Herod
has turned off the Internet and mobile phones, the modem
is useless and the eagles are coming. You go because the
                                                eagles
have died off with the vultures and the ancestors are
                                                angry
there's no one to clean the bones. You go in peace. You
                                                go in war.
Someone has offered you a job. You go because the dog
                                                is going too.
Because the Grand Vizier sent paramilitaries to your
                                                home last night,
you have to go quick and leave the dog behind.

You go because you've eaten the dog and that's it,
                                                there's nothing else.
You go because you've given up and might as well.
                                        Because your love
is dead – because she laughed at you. You go because
                                        she's coming with you:

it will be a big adventure and you'll live happily ever
after.
You go in hope, in faith, in haste; in high spirits,
deep sorrow, deep snow, deep shit and without question.

You pause halfway to stoke up on Omega-3 and horse
shoe crabs.
You go for phosphorus, myrtle-berries, salt. You go for oil
and pepper. It was your father's dying wish.
You go from pole to pole, you go because you can,
you sleep and mate on the wing.
You go because you need a place to shed your skin
in safety. You go with a thousand questions but you are
growing up,
growing old, moving on. Say goodbye to the might-
have-beens –

you can't step into the same river twice.
You go because hope, need and escape
are names for the same god. You go
because life is sweet, life is cheap, life is flux
and you can't take it with you. You go because you're
alive,
because you're dying, maybe dead already. You go
because you must.

Printed in the United States
by Baker & Taylor Publisher Services